MY Disney
STARS AND HEROES 3

Student's Book with eBook

Anna Osborn

Scope and Sequence

Meet our Stars and Heroes!
page 4

Character names	Stars and Heroes song
She's …	I like …
He can …	I can …
She has …	I have …

	Vocabulary	Grammar and communication	Personal and Social Skills	Cross-curricular	Project and strategies
1 **Animal friends** page 10	**Animals** Animal body parts Where animals live	The meerkat uses its legs to jump. Hyenas use their claws to catch food. **Ask and answer about animals (fact files)** What does a lion have? A lion has claws. Where do birds live? Birds live in the forest.	🧍 **Social awareness:** Helping your friends Are you OK? Can I help you? Do you want to play? **Story:** Animal dress-up	🌍 **Science:** The food chain grass, insect, leaf, meat	💻 **Project:** A food chain poster **Presentation skills:** Starting and finishing presentations
2 **Student life** page 22	**School clubs** School classes Places in a school	What time does math finish? It finishes at eleven thirty. What time do they leave school? They leave at quarter to three. **Give directions (school maps)** How do you get to the gym? Go straight, then turn left/right.	🧍 **Relationship skills:** Working as a team How about we find water first? Let's build a den after that! **Story:** Our amazing den	🌍 **Science:** Green energy coal, energy, oil, sunlight	👥 **Project:** An 'ideal school' brochure **Collaboration:** Dividing up tasks Sharing ideas with the group
3 **Help at home** page 34	**Chores at home 1** Chores at home 2 Daily routine	How often do you set the table? I sometimes set the table. How often does he cook a meal? He often cooks a meal. **Ask and answer about routine (planners)** What do you do before/after you take a shower? I brush my teeth.	🧍 **Self-management:** Doing new things I can ask for help. I can practice **Story:** A birthday surprise	🌍 **Technology:** Important inventions cell phones, electricity, fridges, GPS	📋 **Project:** A class survey **Self-management:** Using web diagrams to organize ideas
4 **Our hobbies** page 46	**Hobbies 1** Hobbies 2 Adjectives	I like singing in a choir. She doesn't like reading comics. Do you like making models? Yes, I do. / No, I don't. **Explain why I do or don't like hobbies (activity program)** What do you like doing in your free time? I like reading comics. Why? Because it's cool!	🧍 **Self-awareness:** Following your dream My dream is to play soccer for my country! Keep trying! Follow your dreams! **Story:** Sato's dream	🌍 **Music:** Musical instruments brass, flute, percussion, string, trumpet, wind	💻 **Project:** A movie storyboard **Presentation skills:** Good presenter behavior
5 **Let's cook!** page 58 	**Things in the kitchen** Food 1 Food 2	There's some ratatouille. There isn't any water. There are some vegetables. There aren't any pancakes. a glass of water **Ask and answer about food quantities (shopping lists)** How many eggplants are there? There are some eggplants. How much garlic is there? There's a little garlic.	🧍 **Responsible decision-making:** Fixing problems Let's work together to fix the problem! How about we / Maybe we can take eggplant soup off the menu? **Story:** What's for lunch?	🌍 **Food technology:** Following a recipe cut, fry, peel, stir	👥 **Project:** A recipe **Collaboration:** Making decisions together

Welcome
page 6

Places	Where do you live?	Where are you from?	Social awareness:
Countries	Do you live in a town or the countryside?	I'm from a town in Turkey.	Celebrating differences
	I live in a town. I live with my mom, dad, and two brothers.	Where are your parents from? My mom is from a big city in South Africa.	She's different from us, but we all like adventures!

	Vocabulary	Grammar and communication	Personal and Social Skills	Cross-curricular	Project and strategies
6 Going places page 70	Things in a city, Places in a city, Transportation	Where are you going? I'm going to the airport. Are you going to the market? Yes, I am. / No, I'm not. **Ask and answer about transportation (a survey)** How do you go to school? I go on foot. How does she go to work? She goes by motorcycle.	**Self-awareness:** Learning new things *Can you help me, please? I want to find a video/instructions/pictures.* **Story:** A journey and a surprise	**Technology:** Green transportation *carpool, electric car, green transportation, public transportation*	**Project:** A transportation infographic **Self-management:** Using headings and pictures to make information easy to understand
7 Things at home page 82	Things at home 1, Things at home 2, Things at home 3	Whose key is this? It's mine. Whose scissors are these? They're yours. **Describe the location of objects** The bracelet is on top of the shelf. The keys are inside the cupboard.	**Responsible decision-making:** Using things again *I can fix it! I can give it away! It's good to use things again.* **Story:** Use it again!	**Science:** Electrical circuits *battery, circuit, switch, wire*	**Project:** My ideal bedroom **Presentation skills:** Good presenter behavior
8 On a journey page 94	Things in nature, Places in nature, Weather	There was a mountain. There wasn't a farm. There were some woods. There weren't any caves. **Ask and answer about the weather** Was there a storm / any fog? Yes, there was. / No, there wasn't. Were there any stars? Yes, there were. / No, there weren't.	**Self-management:** Managing your fears *Breathe in. Breathe out. Count to five. I feel calm!* **Story:** An exciting day	**Earth science:** Dinosaurs *footprints, fossils, layer, mud*	**Project:** A comic book story **Collaboration:** Turn-taking Asking others' opinions
9 Telling stories page 106	Characters in a story, Places in a story, Personality adjectives	Mother Gothel was in the tower. She wasn't in the secret garden. Rapunzel and Eugene were in the town center. They weren't in the castle. **Ask and answer about story characters** Was he quiet? Yes, he was. / No, he wasn't. He was handsome but mean. They were loud but funny.	**Relationship skills:** Making friends *I like soccer, but my friend likes dancing. We both like cats.* **Story:** A special box	**Arts:** Fairy tales *characters, problem, setting, solution*	**Project:** A fairy tale **Self-management:** Planning your work

Grammar reference and Picture dictionary pages 118–127

Meet our Stars and Heroes!

1. Look. Do you know any of our Stars and Heroes?
2. 🎧 Listen and point.
3. 💬 Write three clues. Then play *Who am I?*

> I'm friends with a rat.

> Are you Linguini?

Russell W

- He's friends with Carl.
- He likes animals.
- He flies in a house to South America.

Nala 1

- She's friends with Simba.
- She's nice.
- She has a long tail.

Sulley 2
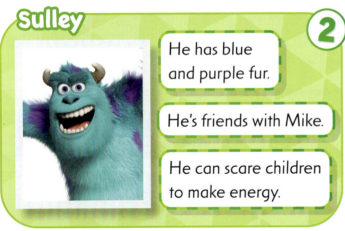
- He has blue and purple fur.
- He's friends with Mike.
- He can scare children to make energy.

Ian 3
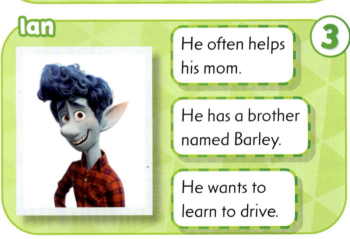
- He often helps his mom.
- He has a brother named Barley.
- He wants to learn to drive.

Miguel 4

- He has a dog named Dante.
- He loves his family.
- He likes playing the guitar.

Linguini 5

- He works in a restaurant.
- He's friends with Remy the rat.
- He can't cook!

Penny (6)
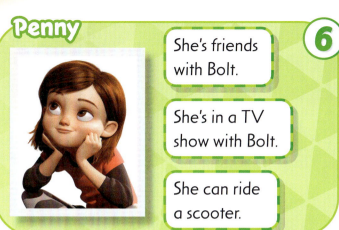
- She's friends with Bolt.
- She's in a TV show with Bolt.
- She can ride a scooter.

Molly (7)
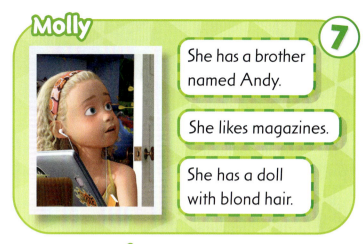
- She has a brother named Andy.
- She likes magazines.
- She has a doll with blond hair.

Arlo (8)

- He can climb mountains.
- He's friends with Spot.
- He sometimes feels scared.

Rapunzel (9)

- She has very long hair!
- She lives in a tower.
- She has lots of different friends.

Sing-along

4 🎵 **Listen and sing.**

Hello, Disney friends!
Hello, everyone!
Welcome, Disney friends!
Let's all have some fun!

Let's travel to new places.
And meet new people, too.
Let's have some great adventures.
We're ready! How about you?

Hello, Disney friends!
Hello, everyone!
Welcome, Disney friends!
Let's all have some fun!

5 💬 **Look and complete for you. Then tell a friend.**

Me!
_____

I have _____
I can _____
I like _____
My favorite Disney friend is _____.

5

Welcome

town

city

LESSON 1 Places

1 🎧 Listen, point, and say. Check (✓) the place you can't see.

2 ▶ Watch the video. Where does Carl live?

3 💬 Draw and play *Guess the place!*

Is it a village?

Yes, it is!

I can name places.

village

countryside

LESSON 2 **Where do you live?**

1. ▶ Watch again. How are Carl and his friends different and the same?

2. 🎧 Listen and write.

   ① Carl lives in a town. Where do you live? Do you _____ in a town or a city?

   ② I live _____ a town. I live with my mom, dad, and brother.

3. 🎵 Listen, chant, and act.

   🎵 Where do you live? Do you live in a town?
   Yes, I do. My house is brown.

   🎵 Where do you live? Do you live in a city?
   Yes, I do. My apartment is pretty!

4. 💬 Ask and answer for you.

   Where do you live? Do you live in a town or the countryside?

   I live in a town. I live with my mom, dad, and two brothers.

I can ask and answer about where people live.

7

LESSON 3
Countries

1 🎧 0.6 **Listen, point, and say. Then tell a friend.**

2 🎧 0.7 **Listen and number.**

3 **Look at 2 and write.**

a He's from ____India____ .
b She's from _____ .
c _____ .
d _____ .

4 💬 **Say for you.**

I'm from Argentina.

I'm from South Africa.

I can name countries.

Hello!

LESSON 4
Where I'm from

1 Look. What animal can you see?

2 🎧 0.8 Listen and read. Who's new?

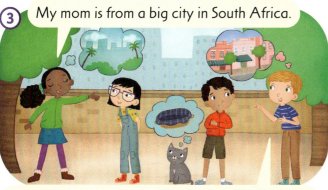

Celebrate differences!

3 💬 Read again and write. Then play *Guess the person!*

~~village~~   countryside   South Africa   United States

1. Sato is from a ___village___ in Japan.
2. Diego's dad is from the _____ in Brazil.
3. Uma's mom is from a big city in _____ .
4. Max is from a town in the _____ .

I'm from a big city in South Africa.

Are you Uma's mom?

4 💬 Ask and answer for you.

Where are you from?

I'm from a town in Turkey.

Where's your mom from?

My mom is from a city in Japan.

Talk buddies

I can say where I'm from.

9

1 Animal friends

How many animal words do you know? Share ideas.

1 Watch the video. Who helps Simba? Check ✓.

1   2   3   4

video story

2 Watch again and answer.

1. How do Simba's friends help him?
2. How does Simba help his friends?
3. How do you help your friends when they feel sad?

LESSON 1 **Vocabulary**

3 🎧 1.1 Listen, find, and say. Then tell a friend.

4 🎵 1.2 Listen, chant, and act.

Animals, animals, we love animals!
There's a hyena! It's gray and small,
There's a giraffe! It's brown and tall.
Animals, animals, we love animals!
There's a rhino! It's big and gray,
There's a meerkat! It stands up all day!
Animals, animals, we love animals!

5 💬 Play *Guess the animal!*

It's small. It can stand up.

Is it a meerkat?

Talk buddies

hyena

rhino

meerkat

giraffe

I can name animals.

11

LESSON 2
Vocabulary

1 🎧 1.3 **Listen, point, and say. Then tell a friend.**

 1 fur
 2 a tail
 3 claws
 4 wings
 5 feathers
 6 a beak
 7 a trunk
 8 horns

2 🎧 1.4 **Listen and put a ✔ or ✗.**

 1
 2
 3
 4

Guess what? An elephant doesn't have horns. It has tusks!

3 Look at 2 and number. Then write.

a It has a big horn and a little horn. What is it? — **2** It's a rhino.
b It has black and yellow feathers, wings, and a beak. What is it? — ☐ _____
c It has big ears and a long trunk. What is it? — ☐ _____
d It has little claws and a long tail. What is it? — ☐ _____

4 💬 **Write three clues. Play *What is it?***

It has a beak and feathers.

What is it?

Is it a bird?

Talk buddies

I can name animal body parts.

12

LESSON 3
Grammar

1 🎧 1.5 **Listen and match.**

1. This bird is flying. Birds use their wings to fly. ☐
2. These birds aren't flying. The elephant uses his tusks to carry his friends. ☐

🎧 1.6 **Grammar Heroes**
The meerkat **uses** its legs **to jump**.
Hyenas **use** their claws **to catch** food.

2 🎧 1.7 **Listen and number.**

3 **Look at 2 and write.**

~~to carry~~   to climb   to eat   to jump

a. Rafiki the monkey uses his hands ___to carry___ Simba.

b. Mufasa the lion uses his claws _____ up the rock.

c. Rafiki the monkey uses his mouth _____ his food.

d. Simba and Nala use their legs _____ in the air.

4 💬 **Choose an animal. Act, say, and guess.**

This animal uses its wings to fly.

Is it a bird?

Talk buddies

I can talk about what body parts animals use to do actions.

13

LESSON 4
Story

Animal dress-up

1 Look. What animals are there?

2 🎧 1.8 Listen and read. What animal does Diego want to be?

① The children are helping at the theater. They find some amazing animal costumes.

"Let's dress up!"

"What's your favorite animal?"

"I want to be a lion!"

② The children choose their costumes.

"Look at me! I'm a lion now. I use my claws to climb! I'm climbing a tall tree in the forest."

③ "I'm an elephant. I use my trunk to drink! I'm drinking water at the lake."

"I'm a bird! I use my wings to fly! I'm flying in the sky."

④ "I want to be a giraffe! It has a long neck!"

⑤ Diego has a problem with his costume.

"The neck doesn't stand up. I can't be a giraffe and I can't play."

"Miaow!"

Think! Look and find. Which animal costume do the children not use?

Go to to page 119 to find out!

14

3 Read again and circle.
1. Uma dresses up as a **lion** / **bird**.
2. Uma uses her **claws** / **tail** to climb.
3. **Sato** / **Max** has feathers.
4. Max uses his **wings** / **trunk** to drink at the lake.

4 Think and answer.
1. How does Diego feel when he can't be a giraffe?
2. What does Max do to help?
3. How do all the children feel at the end of the story?

5 Act out the story. Then reflect.

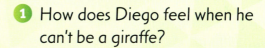

Reflect
One of your friends is sad. How can you help?

Are you OK, Diego? Can I help you?

The giraffe's neck doesn't stand up.

I can read a story about helping a friend.

LESSON 5
Vocabulary and Grammar

1 🎧 1.9 **Listen, point, and say. Then tell a friend.**

1 grassland

2 desert

3 forest

4 lake

5 river

6 ocean

Ways to learn
Water or land?

water	land
lake	

Sing-along

2 🎵 1.10 **Listen and sing. Then match.**

Animals live here, animals live there,
Animals live everywhere!

① Where do meerkats live?
Tell me, tell me, please!
Meerkats live in the forest.
One is walking through the trees!

Chorus

② Where do lions live?
Tell me, tell me, where?
Lions live in the grassland.
One is sitting over there!

a

b

c

Chorus

③ Where do zebras live?
Tell me, tell me, think!
Zebras live near the lake.
They're having a lot to drink!

Chorus

🎧 1.11 **Grammar Heroes**
What does a lion **have**?
A lion **has** claws.
Where do birds **live**?
Birds **live** in the forest.

3 💬 **Choose an animal. Ask and answer.**

Where do zebras live?

Zebras live near the lake.

Talk buddies

I can talk about where animals live.

Extra Lesson

Go online
Phonics

16

LESSON 6
Listening and Speaking

1 ▶ Watch the video and circle.

1. Where do giraffes live? — **grassland / lake**
2. Where does Simba live? — **ocean / forest**
3. What do meerkats eat? — **meat / insects**
4. What does Simba eat? — **meat / insects**
5. What do other lions eat? — **meat / insects**

2 🎧 Listen and complete the fact file.

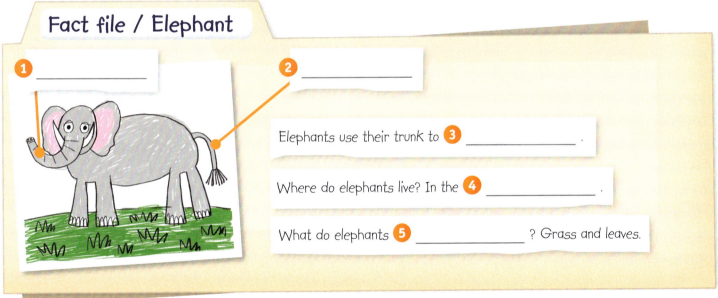

Fact file / Elephant

1. _____
2. _____

Elephants use their trunk to ③ _____ .

Where do elephants live? In the ④ _____ .

What do elephants ⑤ _____ ? Grass and leaves.

Let's communicate!

3 💬 Make your fact files. Ask and answer.

What do lions have?

They have claws and fur.

Go online — Communication Kit

I can use fact files to talk about animals.

17

LESSON 7
Myself and others

Helping your friends

1 Lessons 1 and 4 — 1A — Think and check (✓).

How do they help?	Timon	Max
1 He sings a song.	✓	
2 He tells a story.		
3 He plays with his friends.		
4 He fixes his friend's costume.		

2 🎧 1.13 Listen and circle.

1 Ben **helps** / **doesn't help** Grace and she feels **sad** / **happy**.

2 Ben **helps** / **doesn't help** Grace and she feels **sad** / **happy**.

3 💡 💬 Read, check (✓), and say.

Imagine one of your friends is alone on the playground.

Useful Language
Are you OK?
Can I help you?
Do you want to play?

What can you do?

I play with my friend. ○   I listen to my friend. ○   I share my toys. ○

What can you say?

4 Act out 3 in pairs. Reflect.
- How do you feel now?
- How does your friend feel?

Be a hero!
You have one minute to help a friend! Go!

18   **Social awareness** I can recognize how I can help my friends.

The food chain

LESSON 8
My world

1 Watch the video and circle.

The circle of life means that we **are** / **aren't** all part of nature.

2 **Explore** Read, listen, and draw arrows.

Food chains

Animals eat a lot of different things. A food chain shows what animals eat. A food chain usually starts with the sun and a green plant. The plant uses the sun to make its own food. Some animals only eat plants. Some animals eat plants and other animals. Some animals only eat other animals. You can find different food chains in different places.

leaf — giraffe — lion

Grassland

Here's an example of a food chain in the grassland. The sun makes the **leaf** on the tree grow. The giraffe eats the leaf and the lion eats the giraffe **meat**. The lion is at the top of this food chain.

Forests

Here's an example of a food chain in forests. The sun makes the **grass** grow. The **insect** eats the grass and the snake eats the insect. The snake is at the top of this food chain.

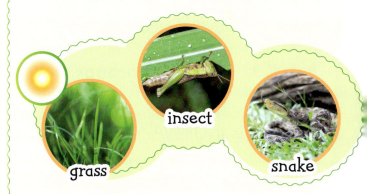

grass — insect — snake

Humans are at the top of lots of food chains, too. Can you think of any examples?

3 **Think** Read again and answer.

1. What does a food chain tell us?
   _____

2. What animal is at the top of the first food chain?
   _____

3. What does the snake eat in the second food chain?
   _____

Try it!
Can you think of a food chain you're part of?

I can read and talk about food chains.

19

**LESSON 9
Project**

A food chain poster

1 (Review) Listen and write. claws grass ~~grassland~~ hyena zebra

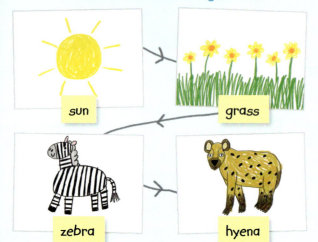

A food chain in the grassland

sun · grass · zebra · hyena

This food chain is in the 1 ____grassland____ .
The sun makes the 2 _____ grow.
The 3 _____ eats the grass.
The hyena has 4 _____ .
The 5 _____ eats the zebra meat.

2 (Get ready) In groups, talk about another food chain.

What is the habitat?   What do animals eat?

What animal is at the top?

This food chain is in the forest. The sun makes the leaves on the trees grow.

3 (Create) Plan and make your food chain poster. **Workbook** page 13

Writing: posters
• Draw pictures and arrows, and write words next to the pictures.

4 (Share) Present your food chain poster.

Tips
Presentation

☐ Start your presentation with:
"Hello, I'd like to tell you about…"

☐ Finish your presentation with:
"Thank you. Does anyone have any questions?"

20   I can make and present a food chain poster.

**LESSON 10
Review**

I can do it!

1 🗨 **Look and write. Then say.**

1. The bird uses its wings to fly.
2. The meerkat _____ _____.
3. The elephant _____ _____.
4. The lion _____ _____.

2 🎧 1.16 **Read and circle. Then listen and check.**

Lucy: Where **1** (do) / does birds live?
Jan: Birds live in trees in the **2** forest / ocean.
Lucy: What do birds have?
Jan: Birds have wings, **3** feathers / fur, and beaks.
Lucy: Where do giraffes live?
Jan: Giraffes live in the **4** lake / grassland.
Lucy: What do giraffes **5** have / has?
Jan: They have fur, long necks, and **6** tails / beaks.

Movie challenge
How many animals from The Lion King can you say in 30 seconds? Go!

Sticker time

I can...
- 🗨 name animals, animal body parts, and places animals live ☐
- 📖 read a story ☐
- 🎨 present a food chain ☐
- 🧍 help my friends ☐

✓ **I completed Unit 1!**

Go online
Big Project

21

2 student life

How many school words do you know? Share ideas.

book club

sports club

dance club

1 Watch the video. What are the games called?

1 Scare Games 2 Sports Games 3 School Games

2 Watch again and circle.

1 Mike and Sulley's team is called the **OKs** / **Monsters**.
2 They **work** / **don't work** as a team in the first race.
3 They **work** / **don't work** as a team in the second race.

video story

22

LESSON 1 **Vocabulary**

3 🎧 2.1 Listen, find, and say. Then tell a friend.

4 🎵 2.2 Listen, chant, and act.

> Clubs, club, clubs are fun.
> There are clubs for everyone!
>
> Cooking club is good!
> Dance club is cool!
> Book club is great!
> Sports club is too!
>
> Clubs, clubs, clubs are fun.
> There are clubs for everyone!

5 💬 Tell a friend about clubs you like and don't like.

I like sports club.
I don't like dance club.

I like cooking club.
I don't like book club.

Talk buddies

cooking club

I can name school clubs.

23

LESSON 2
Vocabulary

1 🎧 2.3 **Listen, point, and say. Then tell a friend.**

 1 math
 2 science
 3 English
 4 music

 5 P.E.
 6 history
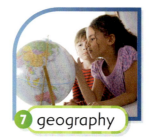 7 geography
 8 art

2 🎧 2.4 **Listen and number.**

a  b 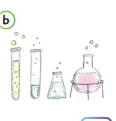 c  d

Guess what?
A quarter of the people in the world can speak English!

3 **Look at 1 and write.**

1 I'm singing in ___music___ .
2 I'm drawing and painting in _____ .
3 I'm learning about the past in _____ .
4 I'm saying three new words in _____ .

4 💬 **Write three clues. Play *Guess the class*!**

I'm playing the guitar.

What class am I in?

Are you in music?

Talk buddies

I can name school classes.

LESSON 3
Grammar

1 🎧 2.5 **Listen and write.** (quarter after eight   eight o'clock)

The class starts at _____ .

Slug gets to his class at _____ _____ . Oh, no!

🎧 2.6 ———— **Grammar Heroes** ————

What time does math **finish**?   It finishes at **eleven thirty**.
What time do the children **leave** school?   They leave at **quarter to three**.

---

2 🎧 2.7 **Listen and match.**

 1 ☐    2 ☐    3 ☐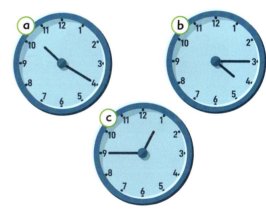

3 **Look at 2 and write.**

1 _What time does_ Mike get to university?   He gets to university at _____ .
2 _____ Sulley have his lunch?   He has his lunch at _____ .
3 _____ Professor Knight's class finish?   His class finishes at _____ .

4 💬 **Ask and answer about your school day.**

What time does math start?   It starts at quarter after eleven.

Talk buddies

I can say what time things start and finish.

25

LESSON 4
Story

Our amazing den

1 **Look. Where are the children?**

2 🎧 2.8 **Listen and read. What are the children building?**

Think!
Look and find. What animal is hiding near the den?
Go to to page 120 to find out!

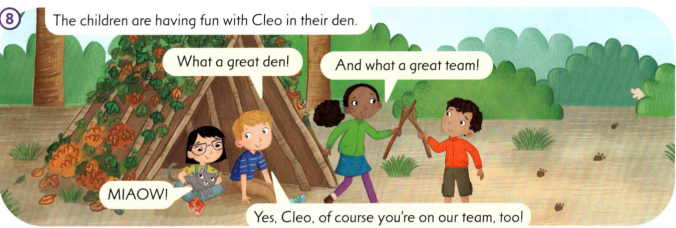

3 Read again and write.

leaves   forest   sticks   ten thirty

1. The children are at _____ school.
2. Sato and Max look for _____ .
3. Diego and Uma look for _____ .
4. The next class starts at _____ .

4 Think and answer.

1. Do the children work as a team at the start and at the end?
2. What does Sato do to help?
3. Do you and your friends work as a team? How?

5 Act out the story. Then reflect.

Reflect
Why is it good to work as a team?

I can fix that. We have to work together.

Yes, I think you're right.

Storytellers

I can read a story about working as a team.

27

LESSON 5
Vocabulary and Grammar

1 🎧 2.9 **Listen, point, and say. Then tell a friend.**

1 sports field

2 library

3 gym

4 computer lab

5 cafeteria

6 science lab

Ways to learn

What do you have at your school?

We have a big sports field at my school.

2 🎧 2.10 **Listen and read. Where are Max and Tina going?**

Max: Hi! Welcome to our school. I'm Max.
Tina: Hey! I'm Tina.
Max: Do you need any help, Tina?
Tina: Yes, please. I want to get some books for history. How do you get to the library?
Max: Go straight, then turn left. But it's lunchtime now.
Tina: Oh, yes. I'm hungry. How do you get to the cafeteria?
Max: Turn right, then go straight. I'm going there now. Come with me. I can show you the way.
Tina: OK, thanks!

🎧 2.11 **Grammar Heroes**

How do you get to the gym?
Go straight, then turn left.
How do you get to the library?
Turn right, then go straight.

go straight   turn right   turn left

3 💬 **Think of a place in your school. Ask and answer.**

How do you get to the sports field?

Go straight, then turn right.

Talk buddies

I can talk about how to get to places in my school.

LESSON 6
Listening and Speaking

1 Watch the video. Check (✔) the places they see on the tour.

library ○
science lab ○
gym ○
cafeteria ○

2 Listen and circle. Where's the library?

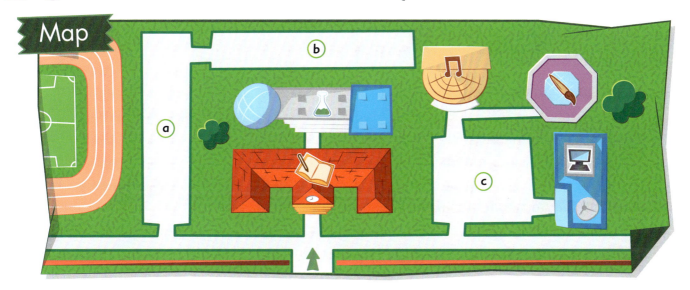
Map

Let's communicate!

3 Look at your map. Ask and answer.

Go online
Communication Kit

How do you get to the library?

Go straight.

I can use a school map to say how to get to places.

LESSON 7
Myself and others

Working as a team

1   **Think and circle.**

1. When the monsters don't work as a team they **do well / don't do well** in the race.

2. When the children work as a team, they **can / can't** build the den.

2 💬 **Look and share ideas.**

a b

Which children are working as a team?

What do you think the message on the poster in b means?

What can you do in a team?

3 **Look and match. Add your ideas.**

1. Listen.
2. Give your ideas.

a. Working as a team!
b. Not working as a team!

3. Don't listen.
4. Help your team.

4 💡 💬 **Read and act out. Reflect.**

Imagine you're at forest school. You have to spend the night in the forest. **Work as a team** to decide what to do.

build a den   make a fire
find water   find food

Useful Language
How about (we find water first)?
Let's (build a den after that)!

Be a hero!
Find one thing you can do in a team that you can't do alone!

• Do you think you are a good team?

30   **Relationship skills** I can work in a team.

Green energy

LESSON 8
Science
My world

1 ▶ **Watch the video and answer.** What kind of energy do the monsters use?

2 🎧 **Explore** Read, listen, and circle.

Energy makes things **stop** / **work**.   Green energy **is** / **isn't** bad for the planet.

What is energy?

Energy makes a lot of our things work. We all use energy every day. Think about your house. Do you have lights or lamps in your rooms? Do you have a computer or a TV? How do you get to school? Do you go by car or bus? All these things use energy.

Where does our energy come from?

We get our energy from a lot of different places. Some of our energy comes from **coal** or **oil**. But these things are bad for the planet. They make the air dirty and they can run out.

We also use green energy. This energy isn't bad for the planet. It doesn't make the air dirty and it doesn't run out.

We get energy from **sunlight**.

We get energy from the wind.

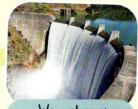
We get energy from water.

We have to start using more green energy. It's good for our planet, and it's good for us, too!

3 💡 **Think** Read again and write.

Green energy	Not green energy
Energy from __sunlight__	Energy from _____
Energy from _____	Energy from _____
Energy from _____	

Try it!
Do you use green energy at school or at home? Find out and tell your team.

I can read and talk about energy.

31

LESSON 9
Project

An 'ideal school' brochure

1   (Review) Listen and circle.

Our ideal school

Our clubs
Cooking club

Our classes
- On Mondays, history and P.E.
- On Wednesdays, ...

Our school building

Green energy

We use energy from sunlight!

At our school we want a **1 cooking / dance** club. We want to have history and **2 science / P.E.** on Mondays. We want to put the **3 cafeteria / library** next to the sports field. Also, we want to use energy from **4 coal / sunlight** in our school.

2 (Get ready) In groups of four, brainstorm ideas for these areas:

Student A: clubs
What clubs do you want to do after school?

Student B: classes
What classes do you want to have?

Student C: places at school
What places are there in your school?

Student D: energy at school
Where does the energy in your school come from?

Tips
Collaboration
☐ Divide up tasks.
☐ Share your ideas with the group.

3 (Create) Plan and make your brochure.

Writing: brochures
- Use headings and pictures.
- Make your school look and sound great!

Workbook page 25

4 (Share) Share your brochure with the class.

I can work in a group to create a brochure for my ideal school.

32

LESSON 10
Review

1 💬 Look and complete. Then ask and answer.

Movie challenge
Close your eyes. What color is Sulley?

1. m<u>ath</u>
2. a_____
3. E_____
4. m_____
5. g_____

What time does math start? — It starts at nine thirty.

2 🎧 2.15 Read and write the places a–d. Then listen and write the places e and f.

cafeteria   computer lab
gym   library   ~~sports field~~
science lab

a ___sports field___
b _____
c _____
d _____
e _____
f _____

ⓐ I play soccer here.
ⓑ I eat my lunch here.
ⓒ I read books here.
ⓓ I learn about energy here.

I can...
- 💬 name clubs, classes, and places in a school ⭕
- 📖 read a story ⭕
- 🎨 design an ideal school ⭕
- 👥 work as a team ⭕

Sticker time

✅ I completed Unit 2!

Go online
Big Project

33

3 Help at home

How many words for rooms at home do you know? Share ideas.

clean the floor

make breakfast

Video story

1 Watch the video. Check (✓) the new thing that Ian wants to do today.

1. feed his pet, Blazey
2. drive a van
3. make breakfast for his mom

2 Watch again and answer.

1. How does Ian feel about learning to drive?
2. How does he feel when he <u>can't</u> drive on the highway?
3. How does he feel when he <u>can</u> drive on the highway?

LESSON 1 **Vocabulary**

3 🎧 3.1 Listen, find, and say. Then tell a friend.

4 🎵 3.2 Listen, chant, and act.

> I help at home every day!
> I can help in lots of ways!
>
> I feed my pet every day.
> I clean the floor. Hooray, hooray!
> I take out the trash every day.
> I make breakfast. Hooray, hooray!
>
> I help at home every day!
> I can help in lots of ways!

5 💬 Act and guess.

Talk buddies

You're cleaning the floor!   Yes, I am!

feed my pet

take out the trash

I can name chores at home.

35

LESSON 2
Vocabulary

1 🎧 3.3 Listen, point, and say. Then tell a friend.

 1 make my bed
 2 wash the dishes
 3 dry the dishes
 4 set the table

 5 clear the table
 6 water the plants
 7 take care of my brother / sister
 8 cook a meal

2 🎧 3.4 Listen and put a ✔ or ✘.

 1
 2
 3
 4

Guess what?
Robots can do lots of housework now. Robots can clean the floor in your bedroom!

3 Look at 1 and write.

All my family help at home. My parents make the food. They **1** ___cook a meal___
for us every night. My sister puts dishes on the table. She **2** _____ .
My brother picks up the dishes from the table when we finish. He **3** _____ .
And I wash the dishes and **4** _____ so they aren't wet.

4 💬 Write three clues. Play *Guess the chores!*

I'm reading a story to Ben.

What am I doing?

Are you taking care of your brother?

Talk buddies

I can name chores at home.

36

LESSON 3
Grammar

1 🎧 3.5 **Listen and write.** (always   usually)

How often does Ian take out the trash?

He _____ takes out the trash.

How often does Ian feed his pet?

He _____ feeds his pet.

Grammar Heroes
🎧 3.6

How often do you set the table?
I **sometimes** set the table.
How often does he cook a meal?
He **often** cooks a meal.

always ● usually ◐
often ◕ sometimes ◔
never ○

2 🎧 3.7 **Listen and match.**

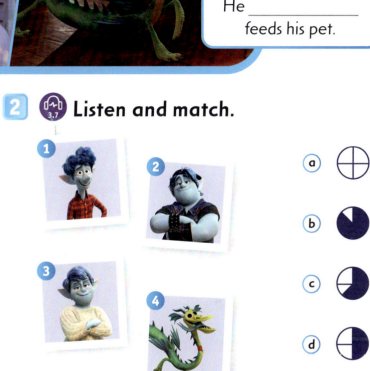

3 **Look at 2 and write.**

1. ___How often does___ Ian set the table? He ___usually___ sets the table.
2. _____ Barley take out the trash? He _____ takes out the trash.
3. _____ Ian's Mom water the plants? She _____ waters the plants.
4. _____ Blazey wash the dishes? He _____ washes the dishes.

4 💬 **Ask and answer about the chores you do.**

How often do you cook a meal?

I never cook a meal.

Talk buddies

I can talk about how often people do things.

37

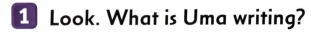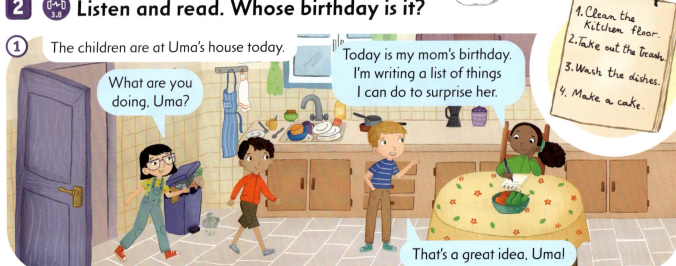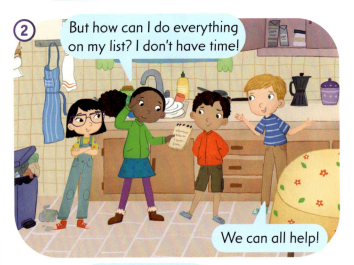

3 Read again and circle *T* (True) or *F* (False).

1. Uma's family helps her. T / F
2. Sato never cleans the floor. T / F
3. Diego always takes out the trash. T / F
4. Max always washes the dishes. T / F
5. Uma can make a cake. T / F

4 Think and answer.

1. Why does Uma write a list?
2. What new thing does Uma do?
3. How does Uma feel after she does the new thing?

5 Act out the story. Then reflect.

Reflect
Why is it good to do new things?

But I never make cake. I don't know how.

It's fun to do new things.

I can read a story about doing new things.

LESSON 5
Vocabulary and Grammar

1 🎧 3.9 **Listen, point, and say. Then tell a friend.**

1 get up

2 get dressed

3 take a shower

Ways to learn

Set vocabulary goals.

Goal: I want to learn three new phrases for things I do in the morning.

4 take a bath

5 brush my hair

6 brush my teeth

Sing-along

2 🎵 3.10 **Listen and sing. Then put a ✓ or ✗.**

We love mornings every day.
We love mornings, hooray, hooray!

What do you do before breakfast?
What do you do every day?
I get up, I take a shower.
Then I get dressed, hooray!

Chorus

What do you do after breakfast?
What do you do every day?
I pack my bag, I brush my teeth.
I brush my hair, hooray!

Chorus

🎧 3.11 Grammar Heroes

What do you do **before** you take a shower?
I brush my teeth.
What does she do **after** she takes a shower?
She gets dressed.

3 💬 **Talk about your morning. Use *before* and *after*.**

I brush my teeth **after** I take a shower.

I brush my teeth **before** I take a shower.

Talk buddies

40 | I can ask and answer questions about the order I do things.

LESSON 6
Listening and Speaking

1 Watch the video and write.

| exercises | ~~gets dressed~~ | makes breakfast |
| plays with his pet |

1. After Ian gets up, he ___gets dressed___.
2. His mom _____ before breakfast.
3. Ian _____ before breakfast.
4. Ian _____ before he goes to school.

2 Listen and number in order.

My Planner

morning

a, b, c, d, e, f

Let's communicate!

3 Complete your planner. Then ask and answer.

Go online
Communication Kit

What do you do **after** you get up?

I always take a shower **after** I get up.

I can use a planner to talk about daily routines.

41

LESSON 7
Myself and others

Doing new things

1 Lessons 1 and 4   **Think and write.**

worried
drive
cake
~~list~~
learn

Both Ian and Uma write a **1** ___list___ of goals (things they want to do). Ian wants to **2** _____ a car and Uma wants to make a **3** _____. They both feel **4** _____, but they **5** _____ how to do their new things.

2 **Read and write E (easy) or H (hard) for you.**

1. Cook a meal for your friends. ____
2. Feed your neighbor's pet. ____
3. Learn a new instrument. ____
4. Get up at 6 o'clock in the morning. ____
5. Read a book every day for a week. ____
6. Try a new food. ____

3 **What stops you from doing hard things? Read and match.**

- I don't know how to do it.
- I don't have time.
- I don't want people to laugh at me.

- It doesn't matter what people think!
- I can learn how to do it!
- I can find 10 minutes a day to do it!

4 **Choose from 2 and share ideas.**

- How can you do it?
- How do you feel when you do a new thing?

I want to learn the piano. But I don't know how to do it. I can learn! My friend Sam can help me.

Useful Language
I can ask for help. I can practice.

Be a hero!
Think of something new you can do to help at home.

Self-management I can learn how to do new things.

42

Important inventions

LESSON 8
My world

1 ▶ Watch the video and answer.

What inventions can you see?

2 🎧 **Explore** Read, listen, and circle.

An invention is a **new / old** idea.

Inventions

An invention is a new thing. People who have ideas for new things are called inventors.

There are a lot of inventions that help us at home. **Electricity** is an important invention. It's a type of energy. This energy makes our lights and machines work, for example, our **fridges** in the kitchen. We can keep our food cold and fresh in the fridge.

Inventions can help us outside the home, too. We use **cell phones** to talk to friends and to send messages. We use **GPS** to find our way when we're traveling.

How do inventors think of ideas for new inventions? Let's ask them.

I start with a problem. I ask: "How can I fix this problem?"

I talk to other people. I ask: "What new thing do you want to help you?"

Think of a new idea! Make a new thing! It's good to try new things. You can be an inventor, too!

Try it!
Think of a new invention for your home. What do you use it for?

3 💡 **Think** Read again and match.

1. We use electricity …
2. We use fridges …
3. We use cell phones …
4. We use GPS …

a. for lots of things, for example, talking to friends.
b. to make our lights and machines work.
c. to find our way on journeys.
d. to keep our food fresh.

I can read and talk about inventions.

43

LESSON 9
Project

A class survey

1 (Review) **Listen and complete.**

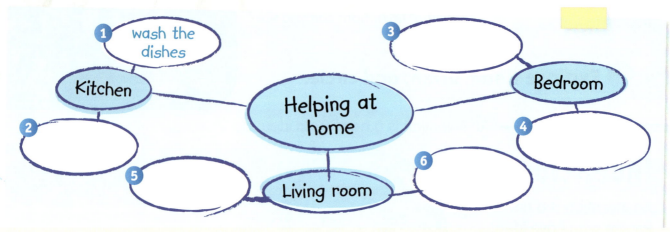

	never	sometimes	often	usually	always
1 How often do you wash the dishes?					

2 (Get ready) **In pairs, think of three chores for each place.**

garden   bathroom   garage

How often do you do these chores?

Tips
Self-management
- ☐ A web diagram is a simple map of ideas with lines and circles.
- ☐ Use a web diagram to organize your vocabulary!

3 (Create) **Plan and write your web diagram and survey.** Workbook page 37

 Writing: survey questions
- Write questions that start with, "How often…?"
- Don't forget to write a question mark (?) at the end of each question.

4 (Share) **Share your survey results with the class.**

Two children always wash the dishes. One child never washes the dishes!

44   I can use a web diagram to create a survey about helping at home.

LESSON 10
Review

I can do it!

1 🗨 Look and write. Then ask and answer.

Malia _always makes her bed_ .   She _____ .   She _____ .   She _____ .

> How often does Malia make her bed?

> She always makes her bed.

2 🎧 3.15 Read and number in order. Then listen and check.

> I sometimes take a bath after I get up. I usually brush my teeth after I take a bath.

Movie challenge
Ian often feeds his pet! What's his pet's name?

 I can...

 🗨 name things I do every day ☐

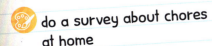 📖 read a story ☐

 🎨 do a survey about chores at home ☐

set goals to do new things ☐

 Sticker time

✓ I completed Unit 3!

 Go online Big Project

45

4 Our hobbies

How many words for hobbies do you know? Share ideas.

watch movies

learn an instrument

Video story

1 Watch the video. Check (✔) Miguel's favorite hobby.

① dressing up ② learning the guitar ③ watching movies

2 Watch again and circle.

① Miguel feels **happy** / **sad** when he plays music.
② Miguel's family want him to **be a musician** / **make shoes**.
③ Miguel's dream is to **be a musician** / **make shoes**.

LESSON 1 **Vocabulary**

3 🎧 4.1 Listen, find, and say. Then tell a friend.

4 🎵 4.2 Listen, chant, and act.

> We like hobbies! Hobbies are cool!
> We do hobbies after school!
>
> I do photography, I dress up, too.
> I like my hobbies! What about you?
>
> *Chorus*
>
> I watch movies, I learn an instrument, too.
> I like my hobbies! What about you?
>
> *Chorus*

5 💬 Act and guess.

Talk buddies

You're learning an instrument! — Yes, I am!

dress up

do photography

I can name hobbies.

47

LESSON 2
Vocabulary

1 🎧 **Listen, point, and say. Then tell a friend.**

 1 play in a band
 2 make models
 3 paint pictures
 4 read comics

 5 go cycling
 6 sing in a choir
 7 write in a journal
 8 make movies

2 🎧 **Listen and number.**

 a
 b
 c
 d

Guess what?
The biggest band comes from China. It has 953 musicians!

3 Look at 1 and number. Then write.

a I ride my bike with my friends. What's my hobby?   [5] I go cycling.
b I write about what I do every day. What's my hobby? [ ] _____
c I like stories with lots of pictures. What's my hobby? [ ] _____
d I use old things to make new things. What's my hobby?   [ ] _____

4 💬 **Write three clues. Play *Guess my hobby*!**

My friends and I make music with our instruments.

What's my hobby?

Do you play in a band?

Talk buddies

I can name hobbies.

48

LESSON 3
Grammar

1 🎧 **Listen and circle.**

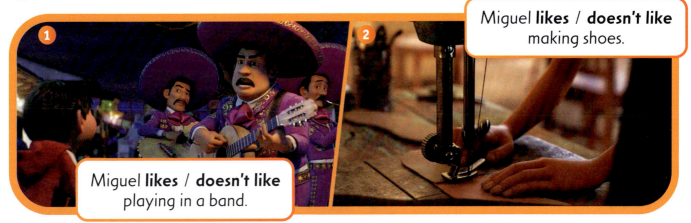

Miguel **likes** / **doesn't like** playing in a band.

Miguel **likes** / **doesn't like** making shoes.

Grammar Heroes

I **like** sing**ing** in a choir.   She **doesn't like** read**ing** comics.
Do you **like** mak**ing** models?   Yes, I **do**. / No, I **don't**.

---

2 🎧 **Listen and draw** 🙂 **or** 🙁 **.**

Matt   Sue

3 **Look at 2 and write.**

① Does Matt ____like____ making models?   No, he doesn't.

② Does he like _____ pictures?   _____

③ _____ Sue _____ reading comics?   _____

④ Does _____ like _____ in a journal?   _____

4 💬 **Ask and answer about your hobbies.**

Do you like making models?   Yes, I do.

I can talk about hobbies I like and don't like doing.

49

LESSON 4
Story

Sato's dream

1 Look. Where does Sato go?

2 🎧 Listen and read. What's Sato's dream?

① The children are talking about their hobbies.

What's your favorite hobby?

I like going cycling.

I like watching movies. Do you like watching movies?

Yes, I do. But my dream is to make movies!

② But I don't know how to make movies.

You have to keep trying!

Yes! Follow your dream!

③ But what can I do?

Oh! You can visit my mom at work. She works at a movie studio. You can learn how to make a movie!

④ The next day, Sato goes to the movie studio.

Hi, Sato! Welcome to the studio. This is Lucy. She can show you how to make a movie.

Nice to meet you, Sato. I'm making a movie with this movie camera.

Wow! This is great! But I don't have a movie camera.

Think!
What's the name of the movie that Lucy is making?
Go to to page 122 to find out!

50

3 Read again and circle.

1. Max **likes** / **doesn't like** going cycling.
2. At the start, Sato **knows** / **doesn't know** how to make a movie.
3. Sato makes a movie with a **movie camera** / **phone**.
4. All the children **like** / **don't like** watching movies.

4 Think and answer.

1. Why does Sato think she can't follow her dream?
2. How does she feel when she can't follow her dream?
3. How does she feel when she follows her dream?

5 Act out the story. Then reflect.

Why is it good to follow your dreams?

But I don't know how to make movies.

You have to keep trying!

I can read a story about following dreams.

LESSON 5
Vocabulary and Grammar

1 🎧 4.9 **Listen, point, and say. Then tell a friend.**

 1 exciting

 2 boring

 3 easy

Ways to learn

Make sentences with pairs of opposites.

It's easy!
It isn't hard!

 4 hard

 5 cool

 6 terrible

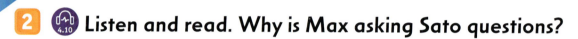

2 🎧 4.10 **Listen and read. Why is Max asking Sato questions?**

Max: I'm writing about our hobbies for the school magazine. Can I ask you some questions, Sato?
Sato: Yes, OK!
Max: What do you like doing in your free time?
Sato: I like making movies.
Max: Oh yes, of course. Why?
Sato: Because it's exciting!
Max: OK, thanks.
Sato: I want to make a new movie.
Max: Really? What's it about?
Sato: It's about our favorite hobbies.
Max: Great! I like going cycling because it's cool. Can I be in your new movie?
Sato: Yes, of course.

🎧 4.11 **Grammar Heroes**

What do you like doing in your free time?
I like reading comics.
Why? **Because** it's cool!

3 💬 **Ask and answer about your hobbies.**

What do you like doing in your free time? Why?

I like dressing up because it's exciting!

Talk buddies

I can talk about why I like doing activities.

LESSON 6
Listening and Speaking

1 ▶ Watch the video. Circle and match.

1. Miguel **likes** / **doesn't like** making shoes because …   (a) it's exciting!
2. He **likes** / **doesn't like** playing with his pet because …   (b) it's hard!
3. He **likes** / **doesn't like** cleaning shoes because …   (c) it's boring!
4. He **likes** / **doesn't like** learning an instrument because …   (d) it's cool!

2 🎧 Listen, draw ☺ or ☹, and write. What does James like doing. Why?

Activities program	Morning	Afternoon
Saturday	☹ because _it's hard._	☺ because _____
Sunday	☺ because _____	☺ because _____

Let's communicate!

3 💬 Use your programs. Ask and answer.

Go online — Communication Kit

- Do you like writing in a journal?
- Yes, I do.
- Why?
- Because it's exciting!

I can use an activity program to talk about what I like doing.

53

LESSON 7
Myself and others

Following your dream!

1 Lessons 1 and 4 **Think and write.** ~~guitar~~ movies musician studio

Miguel likes playing the 1 _____guitar_____ . He loves music. His dream is to become a 2 _____ .

Sato likes making 3 _____ . She loves photography. Her dream is to make movies for a movie 4 _____ .

2 **Read Sato's vision board and answer.**

1. What does Sato like doing?
2. What does she think is exciting?
3. What's her dream?
4. What steps can she take to follow her dream?

Follow my dreams!

I like making movies!

I think drama is exciting!

My dream is to make movies for a movie studio!

1 I can watch lots of movies.
2 I can visit a movie studio.
3 I can make a movie about my friends.

3 **Answer for you.**

1 What do you like doing?
_____

2 What's your dream?
_____

3 How can you follow your dream?
I can _____ .
I can _____ .

Useful Language
My dream is (to play soccer for my country)!
Keep trying!
Follow your dreams!

4 **Share your dream with a friend.**

- Do you have similar ideas?
- Can you help each other follow your dreams?

Be a hero!
Keep a dream journal. Look at it every week!

54 **Self-awareness** I can recognize how to follow my dreams.

Musical instruments

LESSON 8
My world

1 ▶ Watch the video and answer.

How many guitars can you see?

2 🎧 **Explore** Read, listen, and circle.

This article is about different types of **music / musical instruments**.

Musical instruments

Musical instruments come in many different shapes and sizes. Instruments also belong to different musical families. We use different parts of our body to play different musical instruments. Which instrument do you want to learn?

String
A guitar is a **string** instrument. We move our fingers over the strings to play the guitar. Most guitars have six strings.

Percussion
A drum is a **percussion** instrument. We use our hands or sticks to make different sounds on the drum. The drum is a very loud instrument. You can use a drum to communicate with a person a long way away!

Wind
A **flute** is a **wind** instrument. We use our mouths to blow into a flute, and we use our fingers to make different sounds. Some flutes are big, and some flutes are small.

Brass
A **trumpet** is a **brass** instrument. We use our mouths to blow into a trumpet, and we use our fingers to make different sounds. We can make 45 different sounds on a trumpet!

Try it!
Find out about another instrument. What family is it in?

3 🎧 💡 **Think** Listen and complete.

	1	2	3	4
1 What's the instrument?	drum			
2 What family is it in?	percussion			
3 What part of the body do we use to play it?	hands, fingers			

I can read and talk about musical instruments.

55

LESSON 9
Project

A movie storyboard

1 (Review) **Listen and write.**

My movie storyboard: My friends' hobbies

Gabriel likes **1** _____
because it's **2** _____ .

Louise likes **3** _____
because it's **4** _____ .

Theo likes **5** _____
because it's **6** _____ .

2 (Get ready) **Work with two friends. Ask and answer.**

What do you like doing? Why?

I like making models because it's fun.

3 (Create) **Plan and make your storyboard. Then practice your presentation.**

Workbook page 49

Writing: a storyboard
- Write sentences about what happens in your movie.
- Use 'because' to explain the pictures.

4 (Share) **Present your storyboard.**

Tips
Presentation
☐ Speak loudly and slowly when you give a presentation.
☐ Smile and look at your friends when you talk.

I can make and present a movie storyboard about hobbies.

56

LESSON 10 Review

I can do it!

1 💬 Look and write. Then ask and answer.

Rachel _likes_ _painting pictures._

Dan _____ _____.

Sophia _____ _____.

Mario _____ _____.

Does Rachel like painting pictures? *Yes, she does.*

2 🎧 4.16 Read and circle. Then listen and circle.

Meg: What do you like **1** do / (doing)?
Rob: I like **2** make / making models.
Meg: Why?
Rob: Because it's **3** exciting / boring!

Meg likes **4** taking pictures / making movies because it's **5** cool / easy.

Movie challenge
What's Miguel's great grandmother called?

Test your progress with English Benchmark Young Learners

I can...

- 💬 name hobbies and adjectives to describe hobbies ☐
- 📖 read a story ☐
- 🎨 present a movie storyboard about hobbies ☐
- 💡 follow my dreams ☐

Sticker time

✓ I completed Unit 4!

Go online Big Project

57

5 Let's cook!

How many food words do you know? Share ideas.

pan

Video story

1 Watch the video. Who can cook?
① Remy ② Linguini

2 Watch again and answer.
① What problem does Linguini have?
② How do Linguini and Remy fix the problem?
③ How do they feel after they fix the problem?

LESSON 1 **Vocabulary**

3 🎧 Listen, find, and say. Then tell a friend.

4 🎵 Listen, chant, and act.

> Let's cook, let's eat!
> Let's cook, what a treat!
> I have a bowl. I have a pan.
> Can you cook? Yes, I can!
>
> Chorus
>
> I have a cup. I have a plate.
> Let's cook together! It's really great!
>
> Chorus

5 💬 Play *Guess what!*

We put our food on this at dinner time. — Is it a plate?

Talk buddies

bowl

cup

plate

I can name things in the kitchen.

59

LESSON 2
Vocabulary

1 🎧 5.3 **Listen, point, and say. Then tell a friend.**

1 ratatouille

2 strawberries

3 salad

4 pancakes

5 vegetables

6 hot chocolate

7 milkshake

8 water

2 🎧 5.4 **Listen and match.**

Paulo
Lucy Maria

Guess what?
Strawberries can be red, white, purple, yellow, or gold.

3 **Look at 1 and write.**

1 I like tomatoes. Would you like a bowl of r_____?
2 I'm cold and thirsty. Would you like a cup of hot c_____?
3 I'd like a healthy lunch. Would you like a plate of v_____?

4 💬 **Write three clues. Play *Would you like ...?***

I'm hot and thirsty.

I'm hot and thirsty.

Would you like a glass of water?

Talk buddies

I can name food and drinks.

60

LESSON 3
Grammar

1 🎧 5.5 **Listen and match.**

1. There's some ratatouille. There isn't any salad.
2. There aren't any pancakes. There are three bowls of vegetables.

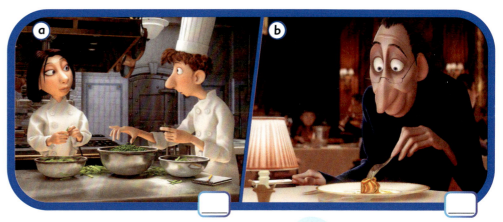

Grammar Heroes

🎧 5.6
There's some ratatouille.   There isn't any water.
There are some vegetables.   There aren't any pancakes.

a glass of water
a bowl of vegetables
a plate of ratatouille

2 🎧 5.7 **Listen and number.**

 a  b  c  d

3 **Look at 2 and write.**

a) There ____are____ some strawberries. There ____are____ three bowls of strawberries.
b) There _____ some pancakes. There _____ two plates of pancakes.
c) There _____ some ratatouille. There _____ two bowls of ratatouille.
d) There _____ some water. There _____ three glasses of water.

4 💬 **Look at 2. Say and guess.**

There are some strawberries. There aren't any pancakes. There are three bowls of strawberries.

It's picture a!

Talk buddies

I can use *there is / are* with countable and uncountable nouns.

61

LESSON 4
Story

What's for lunch?

1 Look. Where are the children?

2 🎧 5.8 Listen and read. What do the children cook?

Think!
Look and find. What can the children make for dessert?

Go to to page 123 to find out!

62

3 Read again and circle *T* (True) or *F* (False).

1. The chef is fine today. T / F
2. The children cook dinner. T / F
3. There are a lot of tomatoes in the bowl. T / F
4. There is some bread. T / F

4 Think and answer.

1. What problem does the man have?
2. How do the children fix the problem?
3. How do the children feel after they fix the problem?

5 Act out the story. Then reflect.

Reflect
How can we fix problems?

Maybe we can help.

Let's work together to fix the problem!

I can read a story about fixing a problem.

LESSON 5
Vocabulary and Grammar

1 🎧 5.9 **Listen, point, and say. Then tell a friend.**

1 zucchini

2 eggplant

3 garlic

4 pepper

5 salt

6 sauce

Ways to learn

Which things can you count?

I can count	I can't count
zucchini	_____
_____	_____
_____	_____

Sing-along

2 🎵 5.10 **Listen and sing. Then match.**

Let's make ratatouille, yum, yum, yum!
Let's make ratatouille! We all want some!

a
c

1 Is there any garlic?
How much can you see?
There's a little garlic.
A little for you and me!

Chorus

2 Are there any eggplants?
How many? Take a look!
There are a few eggplants.
A few for us to cook!

Chorus

3 Are there any zucchinis?
We only need a few.
There are a lot of zucchinis.
A lot for me and you!

🎧 5.11 **Grammar Heroes**

How many eggplants **are there**?
There are a lot of / some / a few eggplants.

How much garlic **is there**?
There's a lot of / some / a little garlic.

3 💬 **Look at 2. Ask and answer.**

How many eggplants are there?

There are a few eggplants.

Talk buddies

64 | I can ask and answer questions with *how much* and *how many*.

Extra Lesson >>>>> Go online Phonics

LESSON 6
Listening and Speaking

1 ▶ Watch the video and circle.

1. How **many** / **much** grapes are there in the bowl?
   There are **a lot of** / **a few** grapes.

2. How **many** / **much** zucchinis are there?
   There are **a lot of** / **a few** zucchinis.

3. How **many** / **much** garlic is there?
   There's **a lot of** / **a little** garlic.

2 🎧 Listen and check (✓). What food do the children want to buy?

Shopping list
- zucchinis ◯
- eggplants ◯
- tomato sauce ◯
- garlic ◯

Let's communicate!

3 💬 Look at your fridge. Ask and answer. What food do you want to buy?

Go online — **Communication Kit**

How many zucchinis are there?

There are a few zucchinis.

I can ask and answer questions with *how much* / *how many*.

65

LESSON 7
Myself and others

Fixing problems

1 [Lessons 1 and 4]   **Think and circle.**

Linguini's problem is that he can't cook Remy's **1 soup / bread**.

2 Remy / The chef teaches Linguini how to cook.

The restaurant's problem is that the **3 chef / rat** is sick.

The children cook **4 soup / ratatouille** for lunch.

2 **Look and complete. What's the problem in this school?**

SCHOOL MENU

		How many portions do we...		
		make?	eat?	throw away?
Sandwiches and soups				
	Chicken sandwich	25	22	(a) 3
	Eggplant soup	25	10	(b)
Hot meals				
	Pasta with tomato sauce	50	8	(c)
	Noodles with vegetables	50	23	(d)
Desserts				
	Chocolate pancakes	75	75	(e)
	Fruit salad	75	28	(f)

3 **Look at 2 and share ideas. Then change the numbers on the school menu.**

How can you fix the problem?

How many portions do you want to make?

Useful Language
Let's fix the problem!
How about we (take soup off the menu)?
Maybe we can (make 30 fruit salads)?

4 **Reflect with a friend.**

• How do you feel about fixing this problem?

Be a hero!
Share and fix a problem with a friend.

Responsible decision-making: I can fix problems.

66

Following a recipe

LESSON 8
My world

1 ▶ Watch the video and answer.

What's Remy cooking for Ego?

2 🎧 **Explore** Read, listen, and circle.

A recipe tells you **how to cook a meal** / **the food you can have in a café**.

Ratatouille

Today you're cooking ratatouille. It's a healthy and delicious meal with lots of fresh vegetables.

A few things to remember in the kitchen:
- Wash your hands with soap before you start.
- Wash all the vegetables in cold water.
- Follow the recipe.
- Be careful when you cut the vegetables.
- Wash the dishes in hot water when you finish.

Good luck!

Ingredients

1 tablespoon of olive oil	2 large zucchinis
1 large onion	3 large bell peppers
3 cloves of garlic	6 tomatoes
1 large eggplant	salt and pepper

1 First, **peel** and **cut** the onion. **Fry** it in the pan with the olive oil for about five minutes. Next, peel and cut the garlic and put it in the pan. Cook for another minute.

2 Cut the eggplants, zucchinis, bell peppers, and tomatoes. Then, add them to the pan and **stir** everything together. Add salt and pepper.

3 Cook the ratatouille for 20 minutes until all the vegetables are soft.

Enjoy your ratatouille with some rice or fresh bread!

3 💡 **Think** Read again, number, and write. Then say.

Try it!
Find a recipe that you want to cook. Tell your friend how to cook it.

a

b

c

d

First, peel the onion.

Then, … Next, …
Finally, …

_____ _____ _peel_ _____

I can understand a recipe.

67

LESSON 9
Project

A recipe

1 (Review) Listen and circle.

1 (Vegetable soup) / pasta and eggplants

Ingredients
8 zucchinis
3 eggplants
1 clove of garlic
1 tablespoon of olive oil

Steps
① Wash and cut the **2** zucchinis / onions and eggplants and then place them in a bowl.
② Peel and cut the garlic. Fry it in a **3** pan / bowl with the oil for 1 minute.
③ Add the vegetables to the **4** plate / pan and fry for about 20 minutes until they are soft.
④ Add hot water and salt and **5** pepper / oil.
⑤ Eat with some fresh bread!

2 (Get ready) In your group, make decisions about:

What recipe to cook

What ingredients there are

What task each friend can do

Tips
Collaboration
☐ Make decisions that most of the group agrees with.
☐ Vote on decisions by putting your hands up.

3 (Create) Plan and write your recipe.

✏️ **Writing:** recipes
• Write three or four steps so your recipe is easy to follow.
• Make your sentences short and simple.

Workbook page 61

4 (Share) Share your recipe with the class.

68   I can work in a group to create a recipe.

LESSON 10
Review

I can do it!

1 🗨 Look and write. Then ask and answer.

1.

   ⓐ ratatouille — <u>There's some ratatouille.</u>
   ⓑ strawberries — <u>There aren't any strawberries.</u>

2.
   ⓐ hot chocolate — _____
   ⓑ salad — _____

3.
   ⓐ two plates of pancakes — _____
   ⓑ two bowls of vegetables — _____

4.
   ⓐ three glasses of water — _____
   ⓑ two cups of hot chocolate — _____

> Is there any ratatouille?.   Yes, there is.

2 🎧 5.15 Read and draw. Then listen and draw.

Jean: How many zucchinis are there?
Costas: There are a lot of zucchinis.
Jean: How much garlic is there?
Costas: There's a little garlic.

Movie challenge
What's Remy's special recipe?

I can...
- 🗨 name things in the kitchen and food ◯
- 📖 read a story ◯
- 🎨 create a recipe ◯
- 🧍 fix a problem ◯

Sticker time

☑ I completed Unit 5!

Go online
Big Project

69

6 Going places

signpost

sidewalk

1 ▶ 6A Watch the video. Check (✔) who Bolt wants to find.

Penny ○   Mittens ○   Rhino ○

2 ▶ 6A Watch again and circle.

1. Bolt has to learn new things because he's really a **superhero** / **dog**.
2. **Mittens** / **Penny** teaches Bolt how to find food and water.
3. Bolt also learns how to **play dog games** / **make a TV show**.

70

LESSON 1 **Vocabulary**

3 🎧 6.1 Listen, find, and say. Then tell a friend.

4 🎵 6.2 Listen, chant, and act.

*Let's go to the city! Come with me!
Let's go to the city! What can you see?*

I can see a signpost. Let's turn right.
I can see a building. It's big and white!

*Let's go to the city! Come with me!
Let's go to the city! What can you see?*

I can see a sidewalk. I want to run.
I can see a road. This is fun!

*Let's go to the city! Come with me!
Let's go to the city! What can you see?*

5 💬 Play *Guess what!*

You walk on this.   Is it a sidewalk?

Talk buddies

building

road

How many words do you know for places in a city? Share ideas.

I can name things in a city.

71

LESSON 2
Vocabulary

1 🎧 6.3 **Listen, point, and say. Then tell a friend.**

 1 bus station
 2 subway station
 3 airport
 4 gas station
 5 movie studio
 6 RV park
 7 market
 8 circus

2 🎧 6.4 **Listen and number.**

 a
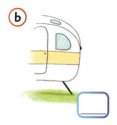 b
 c
 d

Guess what?
New York has 472 subway stations! That's more than any other city in the world.

3 **Look at 1 and write.**

1. I'm waiting for a bus.
   I'm at the _____ .

2. I'm going on a plane!
   I'm at the _____ .

3. I'm looking for a present for my friend.
   I'm at the _____ .

4. My dad is putting gas in our car.
   We're at the _____ .

4 💬 **Write three clues. Play *Where am I?***

I'm making a movie.

Where am I?

Are you at the movie studio?

Talk buddies

I can name places in a city.

72

LESSON 3
Grammar

1 🎧 6.5 **Listen and write.** airport   RV park

Is Bolt going to the _____ ?
Yes, he is.

Where's Bolt going?
He's going to the _____ .

Grammar Heroes 🎧 6.6
Where are you **going**?   **I'm going** to the airport.
Are you **going** to the market?   Yes, I **am**. / No, I'**m not**.

2 🎧 6.7 **Listen and put a ✔ or ✘.**

3 **Look at 2 and write.**

① Where'_s_ she _going_ ?   She'_s going_ to the _bus station_ .
② Where ____ he _____ ?   He _____ to the _____ .
③ Where _____ ?   She _____ .
④ Where _____ ?   He _____ .

4 💬 **Act and guess.**

Are you going to the RV park?   Yes, I am.

Talk buddies

I can talk about where people are going.

73

LESSON 4
Story

A journey and a surprise

1 Look. Where are the children?

2 🎧 6.8 Listen and read. How do the children travel on their journey?

① The children are in town with Max's brother, Tom.

Let's play! Here are your cards. There's a surprise at the end.

Cool!

② My card says, "Read a map and find the bus station." I like learning from pictures and a map is a picture. I can see the bus station here. This way!

③ The children are at the bus station.

My card says, "Read the timetable and take the number 21 bus." Here's the timetable. The number 21 bus is … here! It leaves at quarter after ten. Let's go!

④ My card says, "Buy a ticket." I can't do that. I don't know how to use this ticket machine. It's hard.

⑤ Oh! I can watch that woman buying her ticket. I can learn from her!

Good job, Max!

Think!
Look at the woman in picture 5. What job does she do? Guess!

Go to to page 124 to find out!

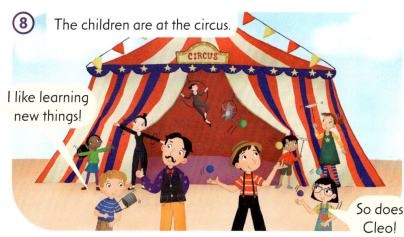

3. Read again and match.

1. Uma learns …
2. Sato learns …
3. Max learns …
4. Diego learns …

a. how to follow directions.
b. how to buy a ticket.
c. how to read a timetable
d. how to read a map.

4. Think and answer.

1. How does Max feel about buying a ticket? Why?
2. What does he do?
3. Why is it good to learn new things?

5. Act out the story. Then reflect.

Reflect
What new things do you want to learn?

I don't know how to use this ticket machine. ... Oh! I can watch that woman... I can learn from her! ...

Good job!

Storytellers

I can read a story about learning new things.

LESSON 5
Vocabulary and Grammar

1 🎧 6.9 **Listen, point, and say. Then tell a friend.**

1 van

2 taxi

3 motorcycle

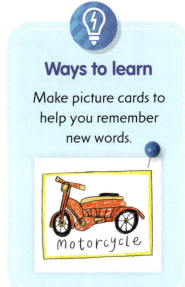
Ways to learn
Make picture cards to help you remember new words.

4 helicopter

5 subway

6 on foot

2 🎧 6.10 **Listen and read. How does Max go to school?**

Max: Hey, guess what! My brother Tom has a new motorcycle.
Uma: Cool! Does he go to work by motorcycle?
Max: No, he doesn't. He goes by subway. He rides his motorcycle on the weekend.
Uma: Oh! How do you go to school? Do you go by motorcycle?
Max: No, of course not! I go by bike. How about you? How do you go to school?
Uma: I go by bus. But one day, I want to get a motorcycle like Tom!

🎧 6.11 **Grammar Heroes**
How do you go to school?
I go **on foot**.
How does she go to work?
She goes **by motorcycle**.

💡 **by** train / taxi / van …
on foot

3 💬 **Ask and answer for you and your family.**

How do you go to school?

I go by subway.

How does your mom or dad go to work?

My mom goes on foot.

Talk buddies

I can talk about traveling to school and work.

LESSON 6
Listening and Speaking

1 Watch the video. Check (✓) the transportation you see.

boat ○ motorcycle ○

bus ○ scooter ○

helicopter ○ subway ○

2 Listen and mark the answers in the survey.

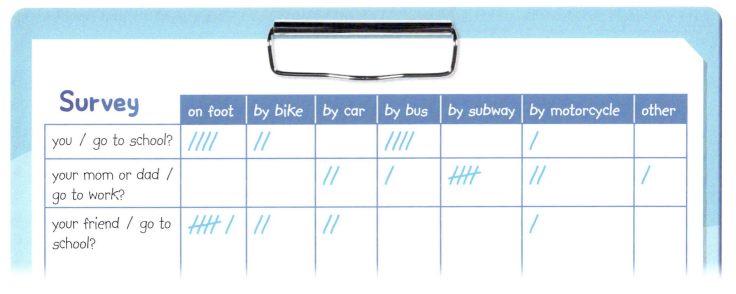

Survey	on foot	by bike	by car	by bus	by subway	by motorcycle	other
you / go to school?	////	//		////		/	
your mom or dad / go to work?			//	/	/////	//	/
your friend / go to school?	///// /	//	//			/	

Let's communicate!

3 Ask your friends and complete your transportation survey.

Go online
Communication Kit

How do you go to school?

I go by bus.

I can do a survey about transportation.

LESSON 7
Myself and others

Learning new things

1 Lessons 1 and 4 💡 **Think and answer.**

① What new things do Bolt and Max learn?

② Do they think it's easy or hard?

③ Do they keep trying or stop trying?

 Max

 Bolt

2 **Follow the chart to find a green box.**

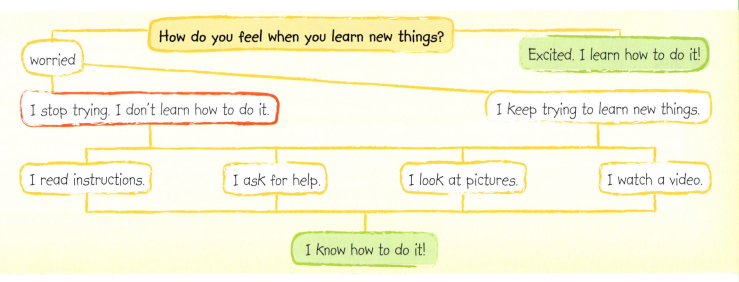

3 💬 **Learn three new words in sign language.**

 please

 thank you

 sorry

Useful Language
Can you help me, please?
I want to find a video/instructions/pictures.

Practice with a friend.   Close your books. Can you remember the signs?

4 💡 **Reflect.**

- How do you feel about learning something new?
- What strategies from 2 do you use?
- What other strategies can you use?

 Be a hero!

Try to learn one new thing every day!

78   **Self-awareness** I can keep trying to learn new things.

Green transportation

LESSON 8
My world

1 Watch the video and answer.

What green transportation does Bolt use?

2 **Explore** Read, listen, and choose.

This article is about…
a) green transportation and clean air.   b) new ideas for green transportation.

Transportation in the future

Using **green transportation** keeps our planet clean. But how can we get everyone to use green transportation? We can make it exciting!

Cars

There are new **electric cars** that don't need a driver. You just put your cell phone in the car and it drives for you. You can still **carpool** in an electric car!

Bikes and motorcycles

We can also use electric bikes and motorcycles. Electric bikes help you to cycle. You can travel a long way before you get tired. We don't see a lot of electric motorcycles on the road right now, but scientists are designing new electric motorcycles for the future.

Public tansportation

Inventors have lots of new ideas for **public transportation**. This bus travels over the road instead of on the road! You don't have to sit in traffic.

This is a green plane that can turn into a green train!

Green transportation in the future looks fun!

3 **Think** Read again and match. Which green transportation do you want to try?

1. There's a bus …   a) that can fly.
2. There's a train …   b) that can drive on its own.
3. There's a car …   c) that goes over cars.

Try it!
Can you use green transportation in your town or city?

I can read and talk about green transportation.

LESSON 9 Project

A transportation infographic

1 (Review) **Listen and write.**

carpool   electric car   ~~on foot~~   public transportation   subway

HOW WE TRAVEL TO SCHOOL

 8 children go **1** _on foot._

 12 children go by bus.

 4 children go by bike.

 2 children go by **2** _____.

 7 children go by car.

Let's use GREEN transportation!

Walk when you can.

Use an **3** _____.

 Use **4** _____.

Ride your bike.

5 _____.

2 (Get ready) **Look back at your survey results in Lesson 6. Answer with a friend.**

Which transport do you use most/least often?

Is it green?

Can you think of a picture to represent each type?

Tips
Self-management

☐ Use headings and short texts with pictures to make information easy to understand.

☐ Use pictures to help you to remember new vocabulary.

3 (Create) **Plan and make your infographic.**

 Writing: infographics
- Write short, interesting headings.
- Don't write long sentences or too much information.
- Make numbers easy to read.

Workbook page 73

4 (Share) **Share your infographic with the class.**

I can make a transportation infographic.

LESSON 10 Review

I can do it!

1 💬 Look and write. Then imagine, ask, and answer.

1. _Where is he going?_ _He's going to the circus._
2. _____ ? _____
3. _____ ? _____
4. _____ ? _____

Where are you going?

I'm going to the movie studio!

2 🎧 6.15 Read and circle. Then listen and circle.

Jean: How **1 do / does** you go to school, Peter?
Peter: I go **2 by / on** bus.
Jean: How **3 do / does** your sister go to work?
Peter: She goes by **4 foot / motorcycle**.

Movie challenge
How many forms of transportation can you remember from *Bolt* in 30 seconds? Go!

1. Laura goes to school by **bus / subway**.
2. Laura's dad goes to work by **taxi / van**.

I can...

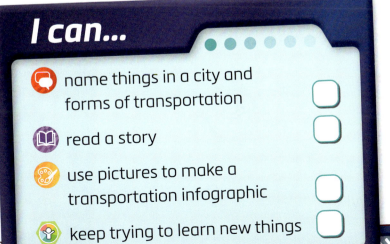

💬 name things in a city and forms of transportation ☐
📖 read a story ☐
🎨 use pictures to make a transportation infographic ☐
🏆 keep trying to learn new things ☐

Sticker time

✅ **I completed Unit 6!**

81

7 Things at home

necklace

How many words for things at home do you know? Share ideas.

Video story

1 🎬 **Watch the video. Check (✔) Andy's favorite toy.**

Woody ◯   Buzz ◯   Jessie ◯   Bullseye ◯

2 🎬 **Watch again and answer.**

1. Who does Molly give her old toys to?
2. Who does Andy give his old toys to?
3. Do you give away your old toys? Why?

laptop

LESSON 1 **Vocabulary**

3 🎧 Listen, find, and say. Then tell a friend.

4 🎵 Listen, chant, and act.

> We use our things every day,
> Our things at home, hooray, hooray!
>
> Here's my magazine. It's cool and new.
> Here's my laptop. It's white and blue.
>
> We use our things every day,
> Our things at home, hooray, hooray!
>
> Here's my toy box. It's square and old.
> Here's my necklace. It's long and gold.
>
> We use our things every day,
> Our things at home, hooray, hooray!

5 💬 Act and guess.   You're using a laptop.   Yes, I am!   **Talk buddies**

toy box

magazine

I can name things at home.

LESSON 2
Vocabulary

1 🎧 7.3 **Listen, point, and say. Then tell a friend.**

 1 earphones
 2 mirror
 3 key
 4 scissors
 5 sunglasses
 6 radio
 7 bracelet
 8 belt

2 🎧 7.4 **Listen and put a ✔ or ✘.**

 1
 2
 3
 4

Guess what?
Buzz Lightyear's belt lights up and makes lots of cool noises!

3 Look at 1 and number. Then write.

a When you see me, you see yourself, too! What am I?
   [2] _a mirror_

b I can cut paper. I can cut string. I can cut everything!
   [ ] _____

c Take care of your eyes in the sun. Put me on and have fun!
   [ ] _____

d Don't drop me on the floor! Use me to open the door!
   [ ] _____

4 💬 **Write three clues. Play *What is it?***

I wear it on my arm.

I wear it on my arm.

Is it a bracelet?

Talk buddies

I can name things at home.

LESSON 3
Grammar

1 🎧 7.5 **Listen and circle.**

Whose key is this?
It's Jessie's key. It's **hers** / **his**.

Whose scissors are these?
They're Woody's scissors. They're **hers** / **his**.

Grammar Heroes
Whose key is this? It's **mine**.
Whose scissors are these? They're **yours**.

💡 mine / yours
his / hers
ours / theirs

2 🎧 7.7 **Listen and number.**

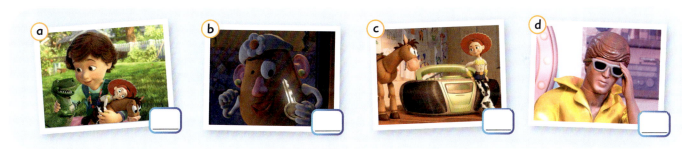

a   b   c   d

3 **Look at 2 and write.**

a. ____Whose____ toys are these? They're Bonnie's toys. They're ____hers____ .
b. _____ key is this? It's Mrs. Potato Head's key. It's _____ .
c. _____ ? It's Jessie and Bullseye's radio. It's _____ .
d. _____ ? They're Ken's sunglasses. They're _____ .

4 💬 **Look at 2. Ask and say.**

Whose toys are these?

They're Bonnie's toys. They're hers.

Talk buddies

I can ask and answer questions about who things belong to.

85

LESSON 4
Story

Use it again!

1 Look. What are the children looking at?

2 🎧 7.8 Listen and read. What does Uma give away?

Think!
Guess how Zoe uses the old things again.
Go to to page 125 to find out!

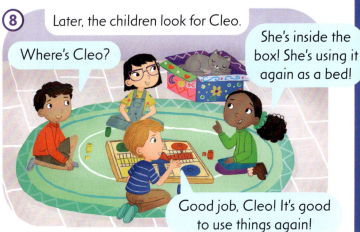

3 Read again and circle *T* (True) or *F* (False).

1. Zoe finds a box of new things.   T / F
2. At first, Uma wants to keep her sunglasses.   T / F
3. Uma often wears the bracelet.   T / F
4. Cleo uses the box again.   T / F

4 Think and answer.

1. Why does Uma give away the sunglasses and bracelet?
2. What do Uma and her friends do with the box? Why?
3. Why is it good to use things again?

5 Act out the story. Then reflect.

Reflect
You have a box of old things. How can you use them again?

Should I put the box in the trash?

No, I can fix it and use it again.

Storytellers

I can read a story about using things again.

87

LESSON 5
Vocabulary and Grammar

1 🎧 7.9 **Listen, point, and say. Then tell a friend.**

 1 cushion
 2 stairs
 3 shelf
 4 cupboard
 5 armchair
 6 drawer

Ways to learn
Put sticky notes on the things in your house to help you remember the words in English.

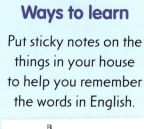

Sing-along

2 🎵 7.10 **Listen and sing. Then match.**

Where are our things? Where, where?
We can't find our things anywhere!

1. Where's my bracelet? Where, where?
   It's beside the cushion over there!

   Chorus

2. Where are my sunglasses? Where, where?
   They're inside the drawer over there!

   Chorus

3. Where are my keys? Where, where?
   They're by the stairs over there!

   Chorus

4. Where's my radio? Where, where?
   It's on top of the cupboard over there!

   Chorus

 a
 b
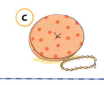 c
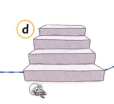 d

Grammar Heroes 🎧 7.11
The bracelet is **on top of** the shelf.
The keys are **inside** the cupboard.

above   below   beside
by   inside   on top of

3 💬 **Look at 2. Ask and answer.**

Where are the keys?

They're by the stairs.

Talk buddies

I can ask and answer questions about where things are.

LESSON 6
Listening and Speaking

1 🎬 **7B** Watch the video. Read and match.

1. Andy's toys are inside …
2. The girl in the armchair is beside …
3. Woody is walking on top of …
4. Woody can fly above …

a. the roof.
b. a cushion.
c. the playground.
d. the box.

2 🎧 **7.12** Listen and match. Where are the things?

Let's communicate!

3 💬 Look at your room. Ask, answer, and draw.

Where's the mirror?

It's above the bed.

Go online
Communication Kit

I can talk about where things are in a room.

89

LESSON 7
Myself and others

Using things again

1 Lessons 1 and 4   **Think and circle.**

1 **Molly** / **Andy** gives toys to Sunnyside.
2 **Molly** / **Andy** gives toys to Bonnie.

Uma gives her bracelet to 3 **Sato** / **Cleo**.
4 **Zoe** / **Uma** and her friends fix the box and 5 **Sato** / **Cleo** uses it again.

2 **Look and write.** Give it away!   Keep it!   Fix it!

3 **Look and share ideas.**

What do you keep? Why?

What do you give away? Why?

What do you fix? Why?

Useful Language
I can fix (it)!
I can give (it) away!
It's good to use things again.

4 **Think of an old thing at home. Use the chart in 2.**

- What can you do with it?
- How do you feel when you use things again?

Be a hero!
Find something old at home. Fix it, paint it, and use it again!

Responsible decision-making I can think of ways of using things again.

Electrical circuits

LESSON 8
My world

1 ▶ **Watch the video and circle.**

Buzz Lightyear works with **coal** / **oil** / **batteries**.

2 🎧 **Explore** Read and listen. Then color and explain.

⚡ **How batteries work**

What is a battery?

We use **batteries** inside lots of our things. Batteries are small objects that make our things work. For example, there are batteries inside cell phones, laptops, radios, and toys. Batteries make these things work because they have energy. There are a lot of different types of batteries. You have to put the right battery inside your things to make them work.

Batteries in electrical circuits.

This is a simple electrical **circuit**. A circuit is a path that energy can travel along. When you turn the **switch on**, you close the circuit. The energy from the battery goes through the **wire** and turns the light on.

When you turn the **switch off**, you open the circuit. The energy from the battery can't go through the wire and so the light goes off.

Look at the circuits. Which of these circuits is working? Color the light that is on. Can you explain why?

The light in picture 1 <u>isn't</u> on because the switch is off.

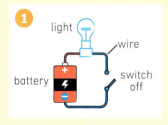
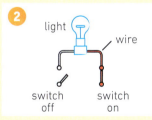

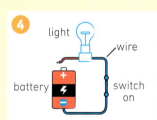

How many things can you think of in your house that use batteries?

3 💡 **Think** Read again and circle.

① Batteries **have** / **don't have** energy.

② An electrical circuit is a path that **energy** / **a battery** travels along.

③ When you turn the switch on in a circuit, you **open** / **close** the circuit and the light works.

Try it!
Find something at home that works with batteries. Press the switch and tell your family about the circuit.

I can read and talk about electrical circuits.

LESSON 9
Project

My ideal bedroom

1 (Review) **Listen and write.**

| by   cupboard   magazines   mirror   ~~beside~~ |

This is my ideal bedroom. My bed is purple. There's a big cupboard **1** _beside_ my bed. My clothes and toys are inside the **2** _____ . There's a blue desk. My green **3** _____ is above my desk. There's a laptop **4** _____ the soft armchair. I keep my **5** _____ in my old toy box! I love my bedroom!

2 (Get ready) **Think about your ideal bedroom. Answer with a friend.**

What things are in your bedroom?

What size are your things?

There's a blue mirror above a pink shelf in my ideal bedroom.

What color are your things?

Where are your things?

3 (Create) **Plan, design, and write about your bedroom.**

Workbook page 85

Writing: a place
- Use the prepositions from this unit: *above, below, inside, on top of, beside, by.*
- Use interesting adjectives.

4 (Share) **Present your bedroom.**

Tips
Presentation
- ☐ Stand up straight when you give a presentation. But try to relax.
- ☐ Point to the picture as you talk about different things in your room.

I can design and present my ideal bedroom.

**LESSON 10
Review**

I can do it!

1 🗨 **Look and write. Then ask and answer.**

1. They're my sunglasses. _They're mine._
2. It's Angela and Peter's laptop. _____ .
3. They're Julie's bracelets. _____ .
4. It's Emilio's mirror. _____ .

Whose mirror is this?   It's his.

2 🎧 7.15 **Read and draw. Then listen and draw.**

Ally: Where's the radio?
Jordan: It's beside the cupboard.
Ally: Where are the sunglasses?
Jordan: They're by the cushion.

Movie challenge
Which toys did Andy give to Bonnie?

I can …

- 🗨 name things at home ⚪
- 📖 read a story ⚪
- 🎨 present my ideal bedroom ⚪
- 🌱 use things again ⚪

Sticker time

✓ **I completed Unit 7!**

Go online
Big project

93

8 On a journey

clouds

How many words for places in nature do you know? Share ideas.

Video story

1 Watch the video and check (✔). Who's scared of everything?

 Spot ○

 Arlo ○

 Poppa ○

 Buck ○

2 Watch again and circle.

1. Arlo's family put their footprints on the wall to show they are **brave** / **scared**.
2. Poppa shows Arlo that the world can be **beautiful** / **scary**.
3. In the end, Arlo **puts** / **doesn't put** his footprint on the wall.

LESSON 1 **Vocabulary**

3 🎧 8.1 Listen, find, and say. Then tell a friend.

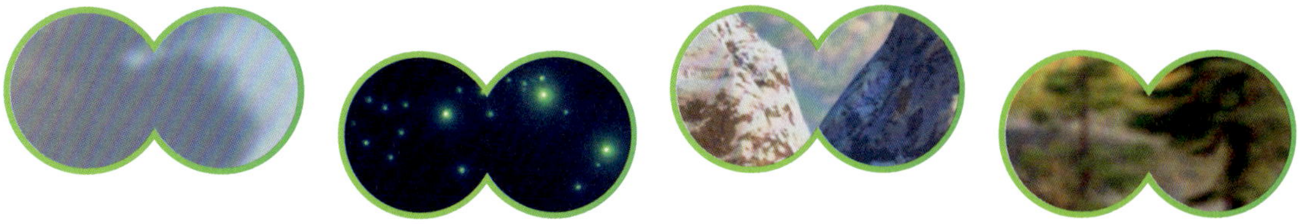

4 🎵 8.2 Listen, chant, and act.

Let's go! Come with me!
Let's go! There's lots to see.

The clouds are white.
And the sky is blue.
The mountains are big.
And the woods are, too.

Let's go! Come with me!
Let's go! There's lots to see.

5 💬 Play *Draw the place!*

Is it the mountains?   Yes, it is!

Talk buddies

woods

sky

mountains

I can name things in nature.

LESSON 2
Vocabulary

1 🎧 8.3 **Listen, point, and say. Then tell a friend.**

 1 field
 2 farm
 3 gate
 4 path
 5 waterfall
 6 valley
 7 volcano
 8 cave

2 🎧 8.4 **Listen and number.**

 a
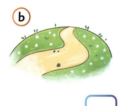 b
 c
 d

Guess what?
The tallest waterfall in the world is Angel Falls in Venezuela. The water falls 979 meters!

3 Look at 1 and write.

1 A ___volcano___ is a mountain that throws out hot rocks and fire.
2 You can open a _____ to walk into a field.
3 A _____ is a place between two mountains.
4 A _____ is a place where farmers grow food or put animals.

4 💬 **Write three clues. Play Where am I?**

It's dark and I can't see.

Where am I?

Are you in a cave?

Talk buddies

96   I can name things in nature.

LESSON 3
Grammar

1 🎧 8.5 **Listen and write.** caves farm ~~mountain~~ woods

On Arlo's journey, there was a ___mountain___ and there were some _____ .

There wasn't a _____ and there weren't any _____ .

🎧 8.6 ---- **Grammar Heroes** ----
There was a mountain.   **There wasn't** a farm.
There were some woods.   **There weren't any** caves.

2 🎧 8.7 **Listen and put a ✔ or ✘.**

3 **Look at 2 and write.**

① ___There was___ a field.
   ___There weren't___ any volcanos.

② _____ a path.
   _____ a waterfall.

③ _____ a gate.
   _____ any caves.

④ _____ a valley.
   _____ some mountains.

4 💬 **Look at 2. Point and say.**

There was a field and a farm. There weren't any waterfalls.

Talk buddies

I can talk about what there was in the past.

97

LESSON 4
Story

An exciting day

1 Look. Where are the children?

2 Listen and read. Who helps Cleo?

Think!
What animal is in the cave? Guess!
Go to to page 126 to find out!

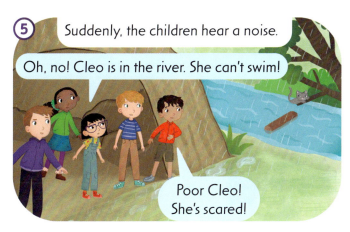

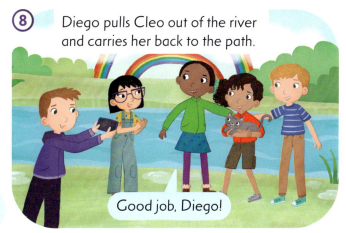

3 Read again and circle.

1. The children see two beautiful **volcanoes** / **waterfalls**.
2. The children hide in a **cave** / **farm**.
3. Cleo falls in the **river** / **waterfall**.
4. Cleo **loves** / **doesn't love** the storm at the end of the story.

4 Think and answer.

1. What is Diego scared of?
2. How does he manage his fear?
3. What does he do at the end of the story?

5 Act out the story. Then reflect.

Reflect
You feel scared. How do you manage your fear?

I'm scared of storms.

Don't worry.

I can read a story about managing fear.

LESSON 5
Vocabulary and Grammar

1 🎧 8.9 **Listen, point, and say. Then tell a friend.**

1 a storm

2 lightning

3 thunder

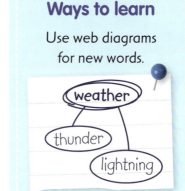
Ways to learn
Use web diagrams for new words.

4 fog

5 a rainbow

6 a star

2 🎧 8.10 **Listen and read. Is Diego scared of storms now?**

Diego: Hey, Mom! Look at this picture of our day in the woods! There was a waterfall and a river.
Mom: Oh, it looks amazing! Were there any gray clouds in the sky?
Diego: Yes, there were.
Mom: Oh, no! Was there a storm?
Diego: Yes, there was. There was thunder and lightning!
Mom: Was there any fog?
Diego: No, there wasn't. But there was a lot of rain. I'm not scared of storms anymore!
Mom: That's great! And look at those colors in the sky!
Diego: Yes, there were two beautiful rainbows and there was a very happy cat!

 Grammar Heroes
Was there a storm / any fog?
Yes, **there was**.
No, **there wasn't**.
Were there any stars?
Yes, **there were**.
No, **there weren't**.

3 💬 **Think about Diego's day in the woods. Ask and answer.**

Was there a storm?

Yes, there was.

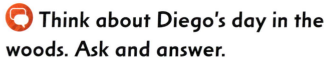

100 | I can ask and answer questions about what there was in the past.

LESSON 6
Listening and Speaking

1 ▶ Watch the video and circle.

1. Was there a big storm?
   (Yes, there was.) / No, there wasn't.
2. Were there any rainbows in the sky?
   Yes, there were. / No, there weren't.
3. Was there any lightning?
   Yes, there was. / No, there wasn't.
4. Were there any boats to help them?
   Yes, there were. / No, there weren't.
5. Was there a waterfall?
   Yes, there was. / No, there wasn't.

2 🎧 Listen and check (✔). Which picture are the children looking at?

1

2

3

Let's communicate!

3 💬 Look at your pictures. Ask, answer, and draw.

Go online
Communication Kit

Were there any clouds?

Yes, there were a few clouds.

I can ask and answer about what there was on a camping trip.

101

**LESSON 7
Myself and others**

Managing your fears

1 ⟵ Lessons 1 and 4 ▶ 💡 **Think and write.**

> dad   friend   breaths   ~~scared~~   walk

Arlo and Diego feel 1 ___scared___ . Arlo talks to his 2 _____ and goes for a 3 _____ to calm down. Diego talks to his 4 _____ and takes deep 5 _____ to calm down.

2 **What do you do when you feel scared? Circle.**

- Talk to a friend
- Draw or color
- Count to five
- Take some deep breaths
- Listen to music
- Go for a walk

3 💡 **Imagine and check (✔).**

Imagine that you feel scared. STOP! Think about your body.

1. I'm hot. ◯
2. I'm breathing very fast. ◯
3. My legs are shaking. ◯
4. I want to cry. ◯
5. My stomach feels funny. ◯
6. I want to run away. ◯

4 **Practice using the calm star.**

- How did you feel before using the star?
- How do you feel after you use it?

Useful Language
Breathe in and out.
Count to five.
I feel calm!

Be a hero!
When you feel scared, use your calm star.

102   **Self-management**   I can manage my fears.

Dinosaurs

LESSON 8
My world

1 Watch the video. Then circle.

Arlo is an **Apatosaurus** / **a Pterodactyl** / **a T-Rex**.

2 **Explore** Read, listen, and circle.

Learning about dinosaurs

We learn about dinosaurs from **fossils** / **mud**.

There were a lot of dinosaurs on our planet millions of years ago. But there aren't any dinosaurs today. So how do we know so much about them? We can find out about dinosaurs by looking at **fossils**. A fossil is the shape of the bones of an animal in a rock.

This is a fossil of a T-Rex. We can see the shape of its strong back legs. This dinosaur can run fast.

This is a fossil of a Pterodactyl. We can see the shape of its wings. This dinosaur can fly.

These are fossils of dinosaur **footprints**.

How do dinosaurs become fossils?

A dinosaur dies and **mud** covers its bones. More mud, sand, and rock go on top of the dinosaur's bones. Over millions of years, the **layers** turn into rock. While this is happening, water gets inside the bones. This creates the shape of a fossil in the rock. Over time, the fossil comes back up to the top of the earth again.

We find new fossils and we learn more about dinosaurs all the time!

Try it!
Are there any fossils near where you live?

3 **Think** Read again and number.

a. Water gets into the bones and makes a fossil shape.

b. The fossil comes back to the top of the earth.

c. A lot of mud, sand, and rock cover the bone. It all turns into rock.

d. A dinosaur dies and mud covers its bones.

I can read and talk about fossils.

103

LESSON 9 Project

A comic book story

1 (Review) **Listen, read, and circle.**

2 (Get ready) **Work in groups to generate ideas about your story.**

Where does your story take place?

Who is in your story?

What happens in each picture?

Tips
Collaboration
☐ Take turns to speak.
☐ Ask others: "What do you think?".

3 (Create) **In groups, draw and write your comic book story.**

✏️ **Writing: a comic book story**

- Write a sentence above a picture to say what's happening.
- Write words that people say in speech bubbles.

Workbook page 97

4 (Share) **Share your comic book story with the class.**

I can work in a group to create a comic book story.

**LESSON 10
Review**

I can do it!

1 🗨 **Look and write. Then ask and answer.**

1. mountains: _There weren't any mountains._
2. woods: _____
3. a cave: _____
4. a farm: _____
5. stars: _____

Were there any stars? — No, there weren't.

Movie challenge
How many places does Arlo see on his journey?

2 **Read and check (✔).**

Elena: Was there a volcano?
Yannis: No, there wasn't. There was a farm and there were two fields.
Elena: Was there a storm?
Yannis: Yes, there was. There was some thunder and lightning. There wasn't a rainbow.

3 🎧 **Listen and check (✔).**
8.15

Sticker time

I can...
- 🗨 name things in nature and weather ⬚
- 📖 read a story ⬚
- 🎨 create a comic book story ⬚
- 👤 manage my fears ⬚

✅ **I completed Unit 8!**

Go online
Big Project

9 Telling stories

How many words do you know for characters in stories? Share ideas.

queen

king

Video story

1 Watch the video. Check (✔) Rapunzel's friends.

1. Hook Hand ○
2. Ulf ○
3. Pascal ○
4. Maximus ○

2 Watch again and answer.

1. How does Rapunzel make friends with the people in the restaurant?
2. How does Rapunzel make friends with the people in the town?
3. What do you like doing with new friends?

LESSON 1 Vocabulary

3 🎧 9.1 Listen, find, and say. Then tell a friend.

4 🎵 9.2 Listen, chant, and act.

> Look at the people in our book!
> Let's read the story! Let's take a look!
>
> There's a king. He's tall and old.
> There's a queen. Her crown is gold.
> There's a princess. Her hair is long.
> There's a prince. He's singing a song.
>
> Look at the people in our book!
> Let's read the story! Let's take a look!

5 💬 Play *Guess the person!*

He has a beard.   Is it the king?

Talk buddies

princess

prince

I can name characters in a story.

107

LESSON 2
Vocabulary

1 🎧 9.3 **Listen, point, and say. Then tell a friend.**

1 in a castle

2 in a tower

3 in a town center

4 in a secret garden

5 in a jungle

6 in a spaceship

7 on another planet

8 on a pirate ship

2 🎧 9.4 **Listen and put a ✔ or ✘.**

? Guess what?
Beauty and the Beast takes place in a castle. It's one of the oldest stories in the world. It's about 4,000 years old!

3 Look at 1 and write.

1. I'm reading a story about an old lady. She works in a store in a ___town center___ .

2. My favorite story is about a frog and a butterfly. They live in a _____ .

3. This story is about a man on a journey on the ocean. He's on a _____ !

4. This story is about an astronaut. She lives on another _____ and she travels in a _____ .

4 💬 **Play** *Where am I?*

Talk buddies

I can see some monkeys.

Are you in a jungle?

I can name places in a story.

108

LESSON 3
Grammar

1 🎧 **Listen and circle.**

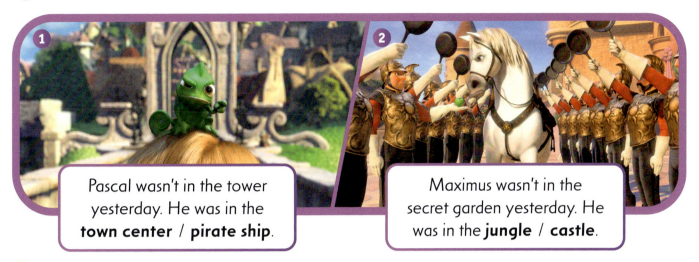

Pascal wasn't in the tower yesterday. He was in the **town center / pirate ship**.

Maximus wasn't in the secret garden yesterday. He was in the **jungle / castle**.

Grammar Heroes

Mother Gothel **was** in the tower.   She **wasn't** in the secret garden.
Rapunzel and Eugene **were** in the town center.   They **weren't** in the castle.

---

2 🎧 **Listen and number.**

a   b   c   d

3 **Look at 2 and write.**

(a) Rapunzel ____was____ in the tower yesterday. She _____ in the jungle.

(b) The king and queen _____ on another planet yesterday. They _____ in the castle.

(c) Rapunzel _____ in the countryside yesterday. She _____ in the town center.

(d) Eugene _____ on a pirate ship yesterday. He _____ in the mountains.

4 💬 **Look at 2. Say and guess.**

Rapunzel was in the tower. She wasn't on a pirate ship!   It's picture a!

Talk buddies

I can say where people were and weren't in the past.

LESSON 4
Story

A special box

1 Look at the first picture. What do you think is inside Zoe's box?

2 🎧 9.8 Listen and read. What do the children make?

1 What's that box, Zoe? — It's very special! Can you guess what's inside? Yes! I know a story about this box from my friend, Li Mei.

2 Li Mei lives in China. We're from different countries and we're great friends! Her story was about a frightening robot in a spaceship. He keeps his space rocks in this box.

3 No! I know about this box from my friend, Pablo. I speak with my mouth but Pablo tells stories with his hands. His story was about a lovely princess in a castle. She keeps her necklaces in this box.

4 No! I know about this box from my friend, Lisa. She's quiet and I'm loud. We're different, but we're good friends. Her story was about a quiet giant in a tower. He keeps his socks in this box.

Think! What's the name of Pirate Zak's pirate ship? Guess!
Go to to page 127 to find out!

110

3 Read again and write.

> giant   ~~robot~~   castle   pirate ship

1. Li Mei's story is about a ____robot____ in a spaceship.
2. Pablo's story is about a princess in a _____.
3. Lisa's story is about a _____ in a tower.
4. David's story is about a pirate on a _____.

4 Think and answer.

How are these people different?

1. Max and Li Mei
2. Uma and David
3. Sato and Pablo

5 Act out the story. Then reflect.

Reflect
Why is it good to be friends with different people?

Li Mei lives in China. We're from different countries, and we're great friends!

My grandpa and I are different ages, but we always have fun!

I can read a story about being friends with different people.

LESSON 5
Vocabulary and Grammar

1 🎧 9.9 **Listen, point, and say. Then tell a friend.**

1 loud

2 quiet

3 lovely

4 handsome

5 mean

6 frightening

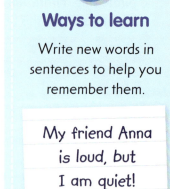

Ways to learn

Write new words in sentences to help you remember them.

My friend Anna is loud, but I am quiet!

Sing-along

2 🎵 9.10 **Listen and sing. Then match.**

We love stories, we love books!
Let's read a story! Let's take a look!

1 There was a princess in the castle.
Her hair was long and black.
Was she lovely? Yes, she was!
She was lovely but loud!

2 There was a pirate on a pirate ship.
His name was Pirate Zak.
Was he mean? No, he wasn't!
He was nice but frightening!

3 There were robots in a spaceship.
Their heads were red and green.
Were they frightening? Yes, they were!
They were frightening but small!

4 There were giants in a tower.
Their socks were always clean.
Were they loud? No, they weren't!
They were quiet but tall!

Chorus

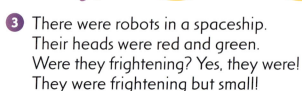
a

b

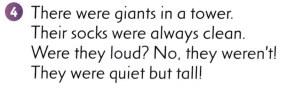
c

d

Grammar Heroes 🎧 9.11
Was he quiet?
Yes, he **was**. / No, he **wasn't**.
He was handsome **but** mean
They were loud **but** funny.

3 💬 **Look at 2. Ask and answer.**

Was the princess lovely?

Yes, she was. She was lovely but loud!

Talk buddies

112   I can ask and answer questions about what characters were like.

Extra Lesson   Go online Phonics

LESSON 6
Listening and Speaking

1 Watch the video and write.

| frightening | handsome | ~~loud~~ |
| lovely | mean | quiet |

1. Hook Hand was ____loud____.
2. Ulf was _____.
3. Mother Gothel was _____ and _____.
4. Eugene was _____.
5. Rapunzel was _____.

2 Listen and check (✔).

Let's communicate!

3 Look at your picture. Ask, answer, and draw.

Go online — Communication Kit

Was the king mean?

Yes, he was!

I can talk about what characters in a story were like.

LESSON 7
Myself and others

Making friends

1 Lessons 1 and 4 🔊 💡 **Think and circle.**

① Rapunzel makes lots of **new** / **old** friends by finding something that they both **like** / **don't like** doing.

② The children in the story are **different** / **the same** in lots of ways but they all love **singing** / **telling stories**.

2 💬 **Talk to three friends. Find things that are the same.**

What sport do you all like doing?

What music do you all like?

What movies do you all like?

What books do you all like?

I like playing basketball. What about you?

3 Now find things that are different. Complete the chart for you and your friends.

	Me	Friend 1	Friend 2	Friend 3
Eye colour?				
Hair color?				
Tall/short?				
Favorite color?				
Favorite animal?				

4 Write one thing that is the same and one thing that is different. Tell the class.

Useful Language
I like soccer, but my friend likes dancing. We both like cats.

Friend 1   Friend 2   Friend 3

same   _____   _____   _____
different _____   _____   _____

Be a hero! Make a new friend in the playground today!

114 **Relationship skills** I can make new friends and be friends with different people.

Fairy tales

LESSON 8
Arts — **My world**

1 ▶ Watch the video and answer.

1. What's the problem?
2. What's the solution to the problem?

2 🎧 **Explore** Read, listen, and circle.

Fairy tales

A fairy tale is a traditional story for children. People often tell fairy tales to their children and pass these old stories down over many years.

Fairy tales often have good and bad **characters** in an interesting **setting**. The bad character usually creates a **problem** for the other characters. The good characters then find a **solution** to the problem and there is a happy ending.

You often find the same characters in fairy tales, for example, a king, a queen, a prince, or a princess. There's sometimes a giant, a pirate, a fairy, a dragon, or a friendly animal, too.

Read this fairy tale:

A fairy tale is an **old** / **new** story.

Once upon a time, there was a tower in a forest. In this tower, there was a dragon called Shadow. Shadow was mean and frightening!

One day, a nice princess called May goes to the tower with her lovely friend, Fred the frog. The dragon wants to eat Princess May. But May is strong and Fred is fast. They chase the dragon. Shadow is scared, and he flies away. Everyone lives happily ever after!

3 💡 **Think** Read again and answer.

1. What's the setting?
   _____
2. Who are the good and bad characters?
   _____
3. What's the problem and the solution?
   _____

Try it!
Find out about a fairy tale from your country. Write the setting, characters, problem, and solution in this fairy tale.

I can understand fairy tales.

115

LESSON 9
Project

A fairy tale

1   (Review) **Listen, read, and complete.**

Once upon a time, there was a pirate ship on the sea. King Marco and Queen Lisa were on the ship. There was a mean pirate on the ship, too.

One day, a lovely princess comes and saves the king and queen. The mean pirate is scared, and he swims away.

They all live happily ever after!

SETTING	CHARACTERS		PROBLEM
1 _a pirate ship_	Good:	Bad:	6 _____
	2 _____	5 _____	
	3 _____		SOLUTION
	4 _____		7 _____

2 (Get ready) **Plan your fairy tale. Talk to a friend about your:**

characters
setting
problem
solution

Tips
Self-management

☐ Plan your story before you start writing it.

☐ Write ideas for the different parts of your story in different boxes.

3 (Create) **Plan and write your fairy tale.**

✏️ Writing: a fairy tale
- Use adjectives to describe the characters in your story: a mean king, a handsome pirate.

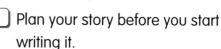
Workbook page 109

4 (Share) **Share your fairy tale with the class.**

116

I can use a plan to create a fairy tale.

LESSON 10
Review

I can do it!

1 💬 **Look and write. Then ask and answer.**

1. king / castle: _The king was in the castle._
2. queen / jungle: _____
3. prince and princess / town center: _____
4. giant / mountains: _____
5. pirates / in a pirate ship: _____

🎬 **Movie challenge**
How many friends does Rapunzel make in the movie?

Was the king in the pirate ship?

No, he wasn't.

2 🎧 9.15 **Listen and circle.**

1. The queen was **lovely** / **frightening**.
2. Was the king frightening? **Yes, he was.** / **No he wasn't.**
3. Were the pirates mean? **Yes, they were.** / **No, they weren't.**
4. The fairy was **loud** / **quiet**.
5. The prince was **handsome** / **mean**.

Test your progress with English Benchmark Young Learners

I can...

 name and describe characters and settings in a story ☐

 read a story ☐

 plan and create a fairy tale ☐

make friends with different people ☐

Sticker time

✓ **I completed Unit 9!**

Go online
Big Project

117

Grammar

1 Asking where people live

Where	do	I you we they	live?
	does	she/he	

I We They	live		in a town.
She/He	lives		in the countryside.

Do you Does he/she Do they	live	in the countryside? in a city? in a village? in a town?
Yes, I do. Yes, he/she does. Yes, they do.		No, I don't. No, he/she doesn't. No, they don't.

2 Asking where people are from

Where	are you is your grandma are your parents	from?
I'm He's/She's They're	from	China. the countryside. a town in Japan.

Are you Is he/she Are they	from	China? South Africa? a city?
Yes, I am. Yes, he/she is. Yes, they are.		No, I'm not. No, he/she isn't. No, they aren't.

Vocabulary

1 🎧 10.1 Places

town

city

village

countryside

2 Countries

1 Mexico
2 the United States
3 the United Kingdom
4 Turkey
5 Japan
6 Argentina
7 Brazil
8 South Africa
9 India
10 China

118

1 Grammar

1 use ... to ...

The meerkat The rhino	uses its	legs to jump. claws to catch food. wings to fly.
Birds Hyenas	use their	

2 Wh – questions and answers

Where	does a rhino do birds	live?
A rhino lives Birds live	in	the forest the grassland. a river.

What	does an elephant do lions	have?
An elephant has Lions have		a trunk. claws.

Think!

Answer: b

Vocabulary

1 🎧 10.2 Animals

giraffe

rhino

hyena

meerkat

2 Animal body parts

fur

a tail

claws

wings

feathers

a beak

a trunk

horns

3 Where animals live

grassland

desert

forest

lake

river

ocean

119

2

Grammar

1 Time

What time	does	math the class	start? finish?
	do	they children	
It	starts finishes	at	nine o'clock. eleven thirty. quarter to ten.
They	start finish		

2 Asking for / giving directions

Use **How do you get to + noun**

Go straight, then turn right.

go straight   turn right   turn left

Think!

Answer: c

Vocabulary

1 🎧 10.3 School clubs

sports club   book club

cooking club   dance club

2 School classes

math   science   English

music   PE   history

geography   art

3 Places in a school

sports field   library   gym

computer lab   cafeteria   science lab

3

Grammar

1 Adverbs of frequency

How often	do you does he/she do we/they	set the table? cook a meal? take out the trash?
I You We They	always usually often sometimes never	set the table. cook a meal.
He/She		takes out the trash.

 always   sometimes

usually never

often

2 before and after

7:00	7:10	7:20
brush my teeth	take a shower	get dressed

What do you do	before after	you take a shower?
I brush my teeth	before after	I take a shower.

Think!

Answer: a film studio

Vocabulary

1 Chores at home 1

take out the trash   feed my pet

clean the floor   make breakfast

2 Chores at home 2

make my bed   wash the dishes   dry the dishes

set the table   clear the table   water the plants

take care of my brother/sister   cook a meal

3 Daily routine

get up   get dressed   take a shower

take a bath   brush my hair   brush my teeth

Grammar

1 *like* + verb + *ing*

I You We They	like don't like	painting pictures. making movies. reading comics
He/She	likes doesn't like	

Do you Do they	like	going cycling? singing in a choir?
Does he/she		
Yes, I do. Yes, he/she does.		No, I don't. No, he/she doesn't.

2 *Why* and *because*

What do you like doing in your free time? I like reading comics.
Why? **Because** it's cool!
What does Max like doing in his free time? He likes making movies.
Why? **Because** it's exciting.

Think!

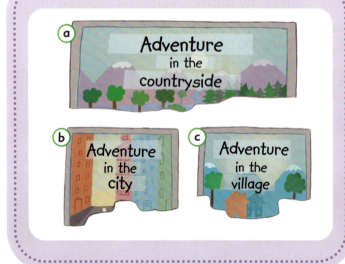

Vocabulary

1 🎧 Hobbies 1

do photography dress up

learn an instrument watch movies

2 Hobbies 2

play in a band make models paint pictures

read comics go cycling sing in a choir

write in a journal make movies

3 Adjectives

exciting boring easy

hard cool terrible

Answer: b

5

Grammar

1 There is/ There are

There's a There isn't a	banana. bowl of salad
There are some There aren't any	strawberries. plates of rice.
There's some There isn't any	pie. water.

2 Questions

Is there any	garlic? sauce?
Yes, there is.	No, there isn't.
Are there any	apples? eggs?
Yes, there are.	No, there aren't.

How much	salt ratatouille	is there?
There's	a lot of some a little	salt. ratatouille.
How many	eggplants pancakes	are there?
There are	a lot of some a few	eggplants. pancakes.

Think!

a   b   c

Answer: b

Vocabulary

1 🎧 10.6 Things in the kitchen

1 pan   2 bowl

3 plate   4 cup

2 Food 1

1 ratatouille   2 strawberries   3 salad

4 pancakes   5 vegetables   6 hot chocolate

7 milkshake   8 water

3 Food 2

1 zucchini   2 eggplant   3 garlic

4 pepper   5 salt   6 sauce

6

Grammar

1 be going to (Present Progressive)

Where	are you is he/she are we/they	going?
I'm He's/She's We're They're	going	to the market. to the RV park. to the movie theater.

Are you Is he/she Are they	going	to the subway station? to the circus?
Yes,	I am. he/she is. they are.	No,	I'm not. he/she isn't. they aren't.

2 Using transportation

How do you How does he /she	go to school? go to work?
I go to school He/she goes to work	by train. by bus. on foot.

Think!

Answer: a

Vocabulary

1 🎧 10.7 Things in a city

1 sidewalk

2 building

3 signpost

4 road

2 Places in a city

1 bus station

2 subway station

3 airport

4 gas station

5 movie studio

6 RV park

7 market

8 circus

3 Transportation

1 van

2 taxi

3 motorcycle

4 helicopter

5 subway

6 on foot

7

Grammar

1 Whose / possessive pronouns

Whose	key radio mirror	is this?
	earphones sunglasses scissors	are these?
It's They're	mine / yours his / hers ours / theirs	

2 Prepositions of place

The picture is **above** the mirror.
The necklace is **below** the shelf.
The sunglasses are **inside** the drawer
The cushion is **on top of** the armchair.
The radio is **beside** the cupboard.
The bracelet is **by** the stairs.

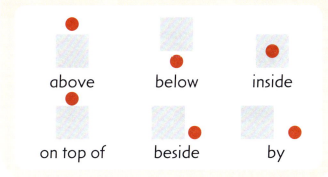

above · below · inside
on top of · beside · by

Think!

Answer: cup – pencil holder, boot – flower pot, piece of material – bag

Vocabulary

1 🎧 10.8 Things at home 1

1. laptop
2. magazine
3. toy box
4. necklace

2 Things at home 2

1. earphones
2. mirror
3. key
4. scissors
5. sunglasses
6. radio
7. bracelet
8. belt

3 Things at home 3

1. cushion
2. stairs
3. shelf
4. cupboard
5. armchair
6. drawer

125

8

Grammar

1 there was / there were

There was a	storm.
There wasn't a	cave.
	path.

There were some	clouds.
There weren't any	stars.
	mountains.

2 Questions

Was there	a rainbow?
	any fog?
Yes, there was.	No, there wasn't.
Were there	any clouds?
	any fields?
Yes, there were.	No, there weren't.

Think!

a
b
c

Answer: a

Vocabulary

1 🎧 10.9 Things in nature

1 clouds   2 woods

3 sky   4 mountains

2 Places in nature

1 field   2 farm   3 gate

4 path   5 waterfall   6 valley

7 volcano   8 cave

3 Weather

1 a storm   2 lightning   3 thunder

4 fog   5 a rainbow   6 a star

126

9

Grammar

1 was / were

He/She The princess The giant	was wasn't	in the castle. in the town center. in the forest. in the spaceship
They The pirates The robots	were weren't	

2 Questions

Was he/she Were they		quiet? frightening?	
Yes,	he/she was. they were.	No,	he/she wasn't. they weren't.

Do you Does he/she	go to school go to work	by train? by bus? on foot?	
Yes,	I do. he/she does.	No,	I don't. he/she doesn't.

But

He was handsome **but** frightening.
They were funny **but** quiet.

Think!

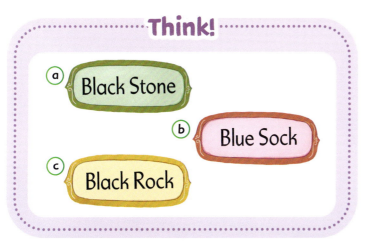

a Black Stone
b Blue Sock
c Black Rock

Answer: c

Vocabulary

1 🎧 10.10 Characters in a story

king — queen

prince — princess

2 Places in a story

in a castle — in a tower — in a town center

in a secret garden — in a jungle — in a spaceship

on another planet — on a pirate ship

3 Personality adjectives

loud — quiet — lovely

handsome — mean — frightening

127

Pearson Education Limited
KAO Two
KAO Park
Hockham Way
Harlow, Essex
CM17 9SR
England
and Associated Companies throughout the world.

pearsonenglish.com
© Pearson Education Limited 2022

© 2022 Disney Enterprises, Inc. All rights reserved. Pixar
properties © Disney/Pixar

The right of Anna Osborn to be identified as the author of this
Work has been asserted by her in accordance with the Copyright,
Designs and Patents Act 1988.

Mr. and Mrs. Potato Head® are registered trademarks of Hasbro,
Inc. Used with permission. © Hasbro, Inc. All rights reserved.
© Just Play, LLC.

All rights reserved; no part of this publication may be reproduced,
stored in a retrieval system, or transmitted in any form or by
any means, electronic, mechanical, photocopying, recording, or
otherwise without the prior written permission of the Publishers.

First published 2022
ISBN: 978-1-292-44170-2
Set in Arta Medium 17/22pt

Printed in Slovakia by Neografia

Acknowledgements:
The publishers and author would like to thank the following
people for their feedback and comments during the development
of the material: Dilek Akin, Burcu Hasbay, Martha Illescas, Maja
Jankovic, Sandy Meza, Monica Medina, Olga Mokrushina, Soledad
O'Keefe, Anita Parlaj.

Image Credits:
123RF.com: Arvind Balaraman 8, Belchonock 48, 67, 122, Choreograph 40, 121, David
Castillo Dominici 19, Graham Oliver 24, 120, Iakov Filimonov 32, Iakov Kalinin 16, 119,
Jakobradlgruber 96, 97, 126, Johan Swanepoel 119, Katarzyna Białasiewicz 52, Kevin
Eaves 6, Lembergvector 33, Maria Wachala 76, 124, Maxpayne222 76, 124, Michael
Rosskothen 108, 127, Mykola Iegorov 6, Panu Ruangjan 12, 119, Rawpixel 24, 120,
Realcg 100, 126, Sergein 51, Sunisa Chukly 84, 125, Tiero 119, Topdeq 16, 119, Vska
54, Wavebreak Media Ltd 56, Wavebreakmediamicro 28, 120; **Alamy Stock Photo:**
Elena Veselova 67, Jose Luis Stephens 76, 124; **Getty Images:** 5m3photos 55, Ana
Silva / EyeEm 60, 123, Andersen Ross Photography Inc 52, 122, Andresr 8, Artur Debat
124, Barry Winiker 76, 124, Ben Richardson 64, 123, Brosa 84, 125, Burazin 123, By
ale_flamy 72, 124, By vesi_127 121, Carlosgaw 64, 123, Carol Yepes 52, 122, Catherine
Delahaye 8, Clare Jackson / EyeEm 60, 123, Courtneyk 80, Daniel A. Leifheit 103, Darrell
Gulin 96, 126, David Papazian 45, Deepak Sethi 99, Deepblue4you 31, Dragos Cojocari
111, DuxX 52, 122, Edwin Remsberg 96, 97, 126, Erik Von Weber 65, FatCamera 39,
120, Flashpop 43, Frank Rothe 48, 122, Fstop123 96, 126, Giulia Fiori Photography
67, GoodLifeStudio 57, Grace Cary 88, 125, Granger Wootz 60, 123, Gremlin 108,
127, Halfpoint Images 36, 121, Harold Carter / EyeEm 84, 125, Hill Street Studios 120,
Hispanolistic 24, Iconogenic 15, Imgorthand 36, 36, 121, 121, Isobel Rees / EyeEm 119,
Jeffrey Coolidge 60, 123, JGI/Jamie Grill 45, 51, 84, John Clutterbuck 97, John M Lund
Photography Inc 63, JohnnyGreig 87, Jose Luis Pelaez Inc 40, 52, 55, 121, 122, Joseph
Clark 64, 123, Juanmonino 48, Jure Gasparic / EyeEm 108, Jurgita Vaicikeviciene / EyeEm
125, Justin Paget 40, 64, 121, 123, Kate_sept2004 121, Klaus Vedfelt 28, 120, 122, 125,
Layland Masuda 41, Level1studio 60, 123, Lorado 127, Martin Diebel 55, Martin Puddy
96, 126, Maskot 124, Mazt Fotografía 12, 119, MirageC 84, 125, Mixetto 24, 120, MoMo
Productions 53, 77, Morsa Images 27, 29, 89, Moyo Studio 48, 122, Narisara Nami 72,
Nitat Termmee 24, 48, 120, 122, Ozgurdonmaz 72, 124, PeopleImages 55, Riska 45, Rob
Lewine 24, 120, Roberto Machado Noa 64, 123, Rushay Booysen / EyeEm 101, Ryasick
124, Schon 126, Schroptschop 31, SDI Productions 68, SEAN GLADWELL 126, Simon
Winnall 77, Siraphol Siricharattakul / EyeEm 88, 125, SolStock 8, 27, 60, StockPlanets
48, 122, Sturti 48, 122, Techa Tungateja / EyeEm 88, 125, Tim Platt 116, Tom Chance
108, Tom Werner 36, 41, 121, Traimak_Ivan 53, 75, Travelpix Ltd 72, 124, Westend61 60,
123, Wyshad Ysh / EyeEm 100, 126, Zhihao 88, 125; **Pearson Education Ltd:** Coleman

Yuen 84, 125, Handan Erek 125, Miguel Dominguez Muñoz 48, 122; **Shutterstock:**
1687018 84, 125, 3Dsculptor 108, 127, Africa Studio 24, 72, 120, 124, Alena Haurylik
60, 123, Andrey Starostin 123, Andrey_Kuzmin 123, Aniwhite 24, 120, Anke van Wyk
12, 119, Ankor Light 124, Anna Nahabed 17, Anton Albert 17, Antonov Maxim 90,
ANURAK PONGPATIMET 122, Bogdan Ionescu 100, 126, Boule 96, 126, Btmedia 124,
Canadastock 118, Carballo 45, ChameleonsEye 101, Coach.vasya 28, 120, Constantine
Pankin 67, DarZel 60, Daxiao Productions 72, DGLimages 40, 121, Dima Moroz 123,
Dmytro Zinkevych 36, 121, Dragonskydrive 84, 125, Dugdax 16, 119, EB Adventure
Photography 76, 124, Elena_prosvirova 40, 121, Ellerslie 108, 127, Espies 75, Fotocrisis
84, 125, Francisehi 12, 119, Gary Saxe 31, Gorodenkoff 28, 120, Haryigit 91, Hxdbzxy
28, 120, Iakov Filimonov 120, Luis Louro 18, 20, 30, 42, 54, 66, 78, 90,102, 114, Inside
Creative House 39, 113, Intellegent Design 90, Jaroslava V 21, Johan Larson 122, Kanea
108, 108, 127, 127, Kavram 100, 126, Kay Cee Lens and Footages 126, Konstanttin 19,
Krakenimages.com 36, 65, 89, 113, Kravik93 127, Lemusique 36, 121, Lifestyle Graphic
66, LightField Studios 12, 127, Lightwavemedia 67, Lineartestpilot 90, Littlekidmoment
78, Ljiljana Jankovic 96, Ljupco Smokovski 54, Lowpower225 96, 97, 126, Luchschen 31,
Luciano Mortula 6, Luiscar74 24, 120, MBI 24, 36, 87, 92, 120, 121, Michael Potter11 19,
Miks Mihails Ignats 6, Milatas 20, Myboys.me 88, 125, Nadianb 60, 123, Haryigit 91, New Africa 36,
121, NiP STUDIO 122, Oleg Znamenskiy 16, 119, Olesia Bilkei 52, 122, Olga Danylenko
126, Ortis 19, Panint Jhonlerkieat 88, 125, Patrick Poendl 16, 119, Patryk Kosmider 43,
Paul Prescott 6, Pavel Chagochkin 108, 127, PEPPERSMINT 96, Photka 20, 32, 56, 68,
80, 92, 104, 116, Plan-B 8, PLANET EARTH 119, Prostock-studio 44, 63, Pwrmc 72, 124,
Rafael Trafaniuc 103, Rafal Olechowski 76, 124, Raksha Shelare 24, 36, Ramon Berk
100, 126, RATOCA 90, Rawpixel.com 122, Richard Whitcombe 118, Rohit Seth 12, S-F
108, 127, Samuel Borges Photography 111, Sanit Fuangnakhon 21, Saurav Pradeep
Dagdelwar 64, 123, Scanrail1 118, Sergey Novikov 121, Sergey Uryadnikov 19, Somyot
Mali-ngam 19, Songquan Deng 118, SpeedKingz 48, 104, 122, Steve Mann 96, 126, Szpeti
100, 126, TECK SIONG ONG 16, 119, TheRealCreator 19, TheVisualsYouNeed 15, Thomas
Dekiere 72, 124, TigerStocks 12, 119, TinnaPong 121, Tracy Starr 12, 119, Travelerpix
72, 124, Tuzemka 29, Valdecasas 12, 119, VaLiza 40, 121, Valua Vitaly 5, 84, 99, Vblinov
12, 119, ViDI Studi 48, Wavebreakmedia 120, 127, XiXinXing 28, 120, YuRi Photolife 103,
Zeber 125.

Illustrations
Laura Borio & Samara Ligia/Advocate pp. 18, 30, 69 (activity 2), 102 (activity 3),
104, 105, 108, 112; **Kay Coenen/Advocate** pp. 79, 91, 101, (online communication
p. 8); **Emily Cooksey/Plum Pudding** pp. 17, 20, 32, 54, 56, 76, 80, 92, 116; **Sernur
Isik/Plum Pudding** pp. 24, 41, 53, 61, 64, 65, 66, 69 (activity 1), 72, 88, 96, (doodles),
(online communication p. 5); **Isobel Lundie/Plum Pudding** pp. 60, 84, 89, 90, 93,
(online communication p. 7); **Emanuela Mannello/Advocate** pp. 113, 115, 117
(online communication p. 9); **Veronica Montoya** (course characters); **Miriam Serafin/
Advocate** pp. 36, 40, 45, 48, 49, 57, 73, 81, (online communication p. 4); **Diego
Vaisberg/Advocate** pp. 8, 21, 25, 29, 33, 102 (activity 4), 103, 114; **Gareth Williams/
Advocate** pp. 23, 35, 47, 59, 71, 83, 95, 107;

Cover illustrations © 2022 Disney Enterprises, Inc. All rights
reserved. Pixar properties © Disney/Pixar